ADVENTURING WITH KIDS

YELLOWSTONE NATIONAL PARK

HARLEY AND ABBY MCALLISTER

MOUNTAINEERS
BOOKS

Mountaineers Books is the nonprofit publishing division of The Mountaineers, an organization founded in 1906 and dedicated to the exploration, preservation, and enjoyment of outdoor and wilderness areas.

1001 SW Klickitat Way, Suite 201 • Seattle, WA 98134
800.553.4453 • www.mountaineersbooks.org

Printed in China
Distributed in the United Kingdom by Cordee, www.cordee.co.uk
First edition, 2017

Copyeditor: Christy Karras
Design and layout: Heidi Smets
Cartographer: Lohnes+Wright
All photographs by the authors unless credited otherwise.
Cover photograph: *Cow and calf bison, Yellowstone National Park* (bretawp/iStock)
Photo on page 6: *Bighorn sheep rams* (NPS photo)
Photo on pages 170–171: *Two girls at Old Faithful* (redhumv/iStock photo)

Library of Congress Cataloging-in-Publication data is on file for this title at https://lccn.loc.gov/2017028624

ISBN (paperback): 978-1-68051-112-3
ISBN (ebook): 978-1-68051-113-0

CONTENTS

Viewing the travertine terraces of Mammoth Hot Springs from the boardwalk (ferrantraite/iStock photo)

INTRODUCTION

Our family has been to Yellowstone National Park a number of times, and each time we began to research which adventures we wanted to tackle in the park, we found it very difficult to find which activities would be enjoyable for kids specifically. There are a number of websites and guidebooks with information about things to do in the park, but children have a different idea of what fun is. For example, Harley will hike for miles just to get a big, beautiful view, but children are more hands-on. They don't care much for views; they would rather interact with their surroundings. Put kids near a creek and they can spend hours along its banks watching the current swirl around rocks, floating stick and leaf boats downstream, building miniature dams and water diversions, or watching the myriad kinds of insect life carry on their activities. And if as adults we thrill at the thought of adding certain iconic animals such as bison or wolves to our bucket list, our children may find just as much joy in watching a playful marmot up close or seeing a relatively common deer wander by their tent. In other words, if you want to make your Yellowstone vacation memorable for your kids, you need to adopt a new outlook on which activities you partake in and how you approach them.

We took it upon ourselves to write this book in the hopes that we can make your big family vacation more engaging, more memorable, and more enjoyable for your kids—and therefore your entire family. A trip to Yellowstone requires a substantial investment of time and money, and it should create a lifetime of memories. You owe it to yourself to make these memories good ones, memories that will bring your family closer together and that you will all look back upon fondly for years to come.

Boardwalks and fallen logs make hiking up Elk Creek more fun.

HOW TO USE THIS BOOK

We have included a number of sights and activities we and our kids have experienced in person, and provided detailed information on how best to enjoy them with a child's perspective in mind. We have also included their locations within the park and in relation to the nearest lodging options so you can spend more time doing things and less time in the car. Keep in mind that Yellowstone is more vast than many other national parks and thus requires careful planning to maximize your time on the trail and minimize your time spent in the car. We've laid out the section of suggested itineraries so that the must-see attractions are organized according to where you're staying.

You'll need to figure out how you're going to get to Yellowstone. There are limitless variations on this, depending on where you live, but it will basically come down to driving in your own vehicle, flying to a nearby airport and then renting a car, or some combination of these that might include renting a recreational vehicle (RV). Each option has implications for how you will approach the question of where you will stay as well.

Check out the map of Yellowstone in the Planning Your Yellowstone Family Vacation section. We have divided the park into regions; every sight or adventure we recommend is listed according to these regions. As you follow the next steps, keep track of which regions feature the things you want to do, as this will ease your planning immensely.

Decide which sights and attractions in Yellowstone you simply must see in order to feel you got the most out of your visit. Our Best Bets chapter will help you with this, but you also might talk to friends or search the internet to get other opinions.

Wherever you hike in Yellowstone National Park, you're bound to find great views from the trail.

Decide how much adventure you want to add to your trip. There are dozens of options for hiking, but there are also a few options for horseback rides, backpacking, canoeing or kayaking, bicycling, or even rafting (just outside the park). We have provided the information you need to choose and book these adventures and have organized this information by region in the Yellowstone Adventures by Region chapter. We review all of these with kids in mind. For each adventure, we offer a quick summary, a time estimate, and then a detailed description of what to expect. We give total (roundtrip) distances for out-and-back hikes and indicate which are loops. Also, we give an idea of how strenuous each activity is so you can plan appropriately based on your personal fitness levels.

Once you've decided which things you want to do, determine where in the park you can do them, group the activities by region, and make your lodging choices accordingly. Each region of the park has both camping and indoor lodging options, so you never have to stray too far from the action. Our Yellowstone Camping and Lodging chapter will tell you what you need to know.

FIVE TIPS FOR MAKING THE MOST OF YOUR YELLOWSTONE FAMILY VACATION

1. Get out of the car.

At 3472 square miles, Yellowstone is a big place (almost three times the size of Rhode Island) with 466 miles of roads. And since there are so many sights to see, it's tempting to simply jump in your car and drive to as many as possible. But don't let this become just another road trip. Yellowstone is essentially a *wild* place, and you should make time to enjoy it as such. Get outside, get off the pavement, and experience the natural as opposed to the manmade. Kids need to experience nature, and the only way to really do it is to get out there. Spend a few nights in a tent, go for a hike on a dirt path, paddle or swim in a natural body of water, get a little dirt under your nails—we tell you how in this book! For many kids, something as simple as this might be the most memorable part of the trip: the time they were even a short distance away from "civilization."

2. Download your digital content prior to departure.

Since Yellowstone is wild, wireless and cellular coverage is spotty or nonexistent. If you expect to use the internet to plan your vacation once you arrive there, you will be out of luck. If you bought this guide as an ebook, be sure to download it to a device before your trip; that goes for any other resources you are using to plan your vacation as well. Some of the lodges do have Wi-Fi access and cell coverage, but it's not something you can count on. This also goes for digital content you may want for your kids while you're driving. You won't be able to stream videos or music for the kiddos while you're there, so download what you think they will need ahead of time. We limit device use with our kids now that they're older and better able to appreciate sights out the window. A good compromise on the device debate is to use audiobooks. You can download digital audiobooks from many places, including for free from your

Junior Ranger patches make great souvenirs.

local library. Your kids have something to listen to, but their eyes are still available for looking out the window.

3. Take advantage of park programs for kids.

The Junior Ranger program is composed of a booklet filled with age-appropriate activities that children complete in order to attain the title of "Junior Ranger." Upon the booklet's completion, a real ranger swears them in as supporters and defenders of the park, and they are given a badge that they can wear proudly. These activities are fun and educational, and they give kids something to do during the inevitable time they will spend in the car or while they wait for you to make dinner. Our kids have enjoyed this program in every park that offers it, and we're sure that yours will too. These packets can be picked up at any visitor center in the park—and the best part is they're free! (The patch shown above costs a few bucks, but they give you a plastic pin for free.)

Another option for those who like to collect things is the Passport to Your National Parks booklet. This small volume is designed to look very much like a traditional passport booklet, and every park has a station at the visitor center where kids can place a stamp from that park in its pages. The stamps are free and the passport booklet costs only $9.95, so it's a great way to commemorate all of the different parks your family has visited. We love to look back at our kids' booklets and remember all the places those stamps represent—and then dream about which park will be next!

4. Start easy and leave extra time.

In the first tip, we encouraged you to get outside, and now we're going to caution you to take it easy. With kids, make your first hike or outing a less challenging one so they don't get discouraged right off the bat. And allow extra time, because while we adults tend to focus on making it to the destination, kids are much more about enjoying the journey. Leave time to take breaks to check out a creek or a flower along the way or do anything else that might pop up. Kids want extra minutes to explore and discover new things, and it's up to you to leave time for this in the schedule.

5. Bring plenty of the essentials.

If a young person is not enjoying himself outside, it's almost always due to one of two things: he is hungry or he is uncomfortable (cold, hot, sore, feet hurt, etc.). Bring a lot of good energy snacks and water. We've lost count of the number of times we've had our kids out and they started whining and getting grouchy, only to take a five-minute snack break and have them back in high spirits and ready to go. So bring plenty of water, trail mix, granola, nuts, fruit, and even candy bars. Napoleon Bonaparte once said that "an army marches on its stomach," and this is even more true of children.

Second, being outside means being exposed to the elements. This brings adventure but also risks, so be prepared. We always carry an extra fleece jacket or sweatshirt with us on even short hikes, and raingear is also a good idea on medium or longer jaunts. Sunscreen is wise, as the elevation in Yellowstone means that more of the sun's ultraviolet rays are making it to your skin than at lower elevations. We have more advice in this book's Safety in the Park chapter, along with more detailed checklists for short walks and long hikes, but food, water, and protection against the elements are always the most important items.

But enough talk. Let's get started! Use the following pages to plan and execute the family vacation of a lifetime.

Hot springs make a dramatic backdrop.

PLANNING YOUR YELLOWSTONE FAMILY VACATION

Planning any sort of trip comes down to a few basic questions: how you'll get there, where you'll stay, and what you'll do while you're there. The last question is made a bit more complicated by the fact that Yellowstone is huge, your time is limited, and your physical abilities will affect your choices, as will your taste for adventure. With that in mind, here is how we suggest you proceed.

First go to the official Yellowstone website and download and print a park map or request that one be sent to you. It's very helpful to have the National Park Service's big fold-out map next to you as you plan. We write all over ours as we make decisions, and it becomes a major part of trip planning. We also "like" the park's Facebook page. This keeps us informed about closures, schedules, activities, and more. Once you've got that out of the way, you're ready to start the hardcore planning!

YELLOWSTONE NATIONAL PARK REGIONS

Yellowstone is roughly a large rectangle with a figure-8-shaped road system covering the park's interior. Visitors enter through one of five different access points: from the south via Grand Teton National Park in Wyoming; from the west via the town of West Yellowstone, Montana; from the north via Gardiner, Montana; from the northeast corner via Cooke City, Montana; and from the east via Cody, Wyoming. If you are coming from a long way away, visit the Getting There section for travel suggestions.

As you plan your trip, it's helpful to think of the park as divided into five general regions (see map below). That way, as you're listing sites you want to see or activities you want to do, you can group them by region and plan to stay nearby to minimize driving time. If you simply choose to stay in one place for the duration of your stay, you can drive to each different region, but be sure you bring your list of things you hope to do that day so you don't arrive back at base camp that evening only to realize that you were close to something you wanted to see but missed it. However, we really don't recommend this strategy for traveling with kids, because it greatly increases the amount of

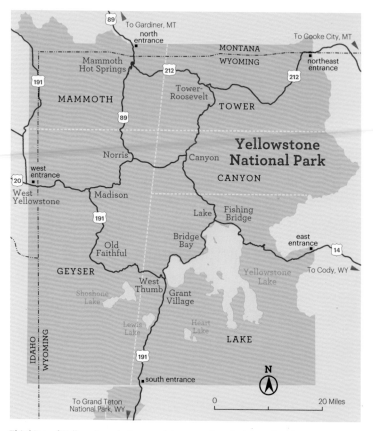

Thinking of Yellowstone in terms of these regions helps make planning easier.

Legend

—(89)—	US Highway	▪	Point of Interest
—(24)—	State Highway	⬢	Campground
———	Other Road	⊕	Restroom
---------	Dirt Road		River
- - - - - -	Trail		Lake
▲	Mountain		Park

car time. Also, arriving back at camp late in the evening means hurried meals, tired kids, and worn-out parents. Although it can seem like a lot of work to move your camp as you start exploring a new region, we think it really works out better for everyone in the end. However you decide to do it, the maps in this guide are designed to help you in your planning.

Yellowstone Regions

GEYSER. The southwest corner of the park, which encompasses the most abundant and impressive geothermal features, including Old Faithful and Grand Prismatic Spring.

MAMMOTH. The northwest corner of the park, including Mammoth Hot Springs.

TOWER. The northeast corner of the park, with abundant hiking opportunities and wildlife.

CANYON. The portion of the park closest to the Grand Canyon of the Yellowstone.

LAKE. Yellowstone Lake and its surroundings.

WHEN TO GO

Since this is a book about going to Yellowstone with kids, we have mostly operated under the assumption that readers will be visiting in the summer months. This is based on a number of factors, including summer vacation from school, historic visitation numbers, and the weather. Kids do get vacation at other times of the year, and homeschoolers have even more flexibility. A visit to the park at other times can be wonderful since the park is less crowded, and the animals may be more active. Our most recent trip was in September, when the crowds had diminished a great deal, and we were fortunate to see many instances of elk rutting behavior that was really exciting.

But that brings us to our next point, which is weather. Even in early September we had a storm come through that left a couple inches of snow on the ground and dropped the overnight temperatures to 17 degrees F. That was a cold night in the tent!

At the end of this section, we have charts of historical temperature data for the park, but keep in mind that these are averages. Daily fluctuations can be much greater.

If you plan a family trip over Thanksgiving, Christmas, or Easter, remember that you will experience winter conditions in the backcountry. Those who enjoy cross-country skiing or snowmobiling know that they require specialized gear and preparation. Judge for yourself what is suitable for your own kids.

The vast majority of families will most likely find themselves planning a summer trip and just dealing with the somewhat crowded conditions at a beautiful and more temperate time of year. With that in mind, here are some specific considerations.

MAY. While most of us think of May as delightful spring weather, in the northern Rockies it is more likely to combine spitting snow or rain with very cool temperatures. You will start to see some wildflowers at lower elevations, but the best show comes later in the year. Temperatures will be on a warming trend, but cold and wet weather will still be common, and mud will dominate the trails. There's a reason elk wait until the first week of June to drop their calves. Conversely, May and early June are good times to see bears, as they have not yet retreated to higher elevations. In early May not all the park's facilities are running, but by the end of the month nearly everything should be open.

Don't forget to get a photo at the big park sign! (Matt and Paula Little photo)

JUNE. In this part of the country, springtime is said to last for about one week in June. We have visited during this time of year and found that while storm fronts can still bring cooler temperatures (or even snow!), they tend to be short-lived and the typical weather pattern is delightful. Animals are active as they make the most of the greening foliage, and the masses of visitors yet to come have not yet pushed them away to more secluded locations. This is also the prime time to see wildflowers.

JULY AND AUGUST. The bulk of people visit Yellowstone between the Fourth of July and Labor Day, and for good reason. In July there are still wildflowers, and the weather is as nice as it gets. Rain can come in afternoon thunderstorms, but this is the best time of year if you want sunny skies and warm days. Trails have dried out, making for good hiking opportunities, and overnight camping is cool but comfortable. As July stretches into August, you start to see fewer wildflowers and the grass dries to a golden brown, but the park is still beautiful.

SEPTEMBER. This time of year marks the beginning of fall and a thinning of the crowds. Weather is still temperate, but you need to be prepared for anything, as cold snaps do happen. The changing colors make for dramatic and beautiful landscapes, and the biting insects are gone. The cooler temperatures can make the animals a little bit more active. By the middle of the month some of the park's facilities are starting to close down—something to be aware of when making reservations.

Yellowstone Weather Averages				
Month	Average High Temperature (F)	Average Low Temperature (F)	Average Precipitation Rain (inches)	Average Precipitation Snow (inches)
January	29	10	1.05	14.6
February	34	13	0.7	9.7
March	40	18	1.05	12.6
April	49	26	1.18	6.0
May	60	34	1.94	1.5
June	69	41	2.07	0
July	80	47	1.43	0
August	79	45	1.34	0
September	68	37	1.23	0.5
October	55	29	1.0	3.3
November	40	19	1.02	9.5
December	30	12	0.96	13.0

GETTING THERE

How you get to the park depends on your preferences and how far away you live from it. Nonetheless, we will offer some things to consider and guidelines to assist in your planning.

Because the park is so large and there is no true bus service to the different areas, you're going to need transportation not only to get to the park but also to get around once inside it. You will also need a place to stay each night and ways to eat inside the park. Given these requirements, you have some different options.

Drive your own car

This is the most obvious choice, as it provides your transportation both to and within the park. Expand meal options beyond eating at restaurants by bringing a camping stove and a cooler (ice is available at many general stores in the park). And you can choose campsites or lodges for sleeping, depending on your tastes and budget. Driving your own car is usually the cheapest option as well, but if your group is small and coming from far away, flying to a nearby city and then renting a vehicle may actually be less expensive. Use a mapping service like Google Maps to find the driving distance to the park, figure the miles per gallon for your vehicle, and research gasoline prices in order to compare these costs to those of flying in and renting a vehicle.

PROS: Maximum flexibility and the ability to bring everything you can fit in your car.

CONS: Potential loss of vacation days to driving, and the expense of staying in hotels along the way.

Rent an RV

Several companies rent RVs (recreational vehicles, a.k.a. motor homes or campervans). While we have never done this ourselves, we are intrigued by the advantages this approach affords. For example, your accommodations travel with you wherever you are. You always have a place to prepare inexpensive meals. You can camp in the more basic campgrounds

WINTER VISITS TO YELLOWSTONE

The average elevation in Yellowstone is 8000 feet. Combine that with its northerly latitude and you can imagine that it is a pretty harsh environment in the winter. While this creates challenges, it also produces a particular type of beauty that can only be found in the austere landscapes winter has to offer. This is especially true in Yellowstone, where warm temperatures below the earth's surface create unique geothermal features when they combine with the frigid temperatures above it. Despite these amazing sights, winter in Yellowstone is not for the timid or unprepared.

The average daily low temperature between October and April is below freezing—and the average daily *high* is below freezing in December and January. Obviously, you can expect a good bit of snow in any of these months.

Traveling with children in winter can be particularly challenging because their smaller size makes it harder for them to maintain body

Frosty bison

temperature, so excursions outside your vehicle will need to be short unless they have some of the best winter clothing.

Almost all of the roads in the park are closed to cars from early November through mid-April. The one exception is the road between Mammoth Hot Springs and the park's Northeast Entrance. However, the only way to get on this road is through the North Entrance near Gardiner, Montana, and Mammoth Hot Springs, because the highways outside the park that lead to the Northeast Entrance are also closed in winter. You can enter Yellowstone through other entrances in the winter, but not by car!

Your options for staying inside the park are also limited because only a single campground, Mammoth Hot Springs, stays open year-round, and many of the lodges are closed during the winter. The available lodging options inside the park are the Mammoth Hot Springs Hotel (currently closed for renovations December–February) and the Old Faithful Snow Lodge and Cabins, but you will need a snowmobile or snowcoach to get you to Old Faithful.

About a dozen different companies offer guided snowmobile and snowcoach tours from mid-December to mid-March, provided there is adequate snow on the roads. Contact information for these operators can change, so find the latest information on the park's website. If you have your own snowmobiles, you can also go unguided on your own, but the rules governing motorized vehicles in winter change frequently, so again, check the park's website for more information.

In summary: if you want to see Yellowstone in the winter, it comes down to two options. First, you can spend a day driving the road between Mammoth and the Northeast Entrance, watching for wildlife and taking short excursions if you have good winter clothes. This portion of the park is the lowest in elevation, so many of the large mammals winter in these areas. Second, you can go all in and stay in a lodge or hotel in a neighboring town and see the park with guided snowmobile or snowcoach excursions. Those who have snowshoes or cross-country skis will be able to access trails and see some unique places in the park, but we have found that these activities are beyond the abilities of all but the most adventurous and well-equipped families.

and still be comfortable. And you don't lose time making and breaking camp when you move, because you don't have to set up tents, put away sleeping bags and pads, etc. You can rent large RVs for a lot of space but with less fuel economy and more difficult campsite selection, or get a smaller van that is more economical and easier to drive but might feel a bit more cramped. You will have to pay campground fees when you park at night, but you will also have a comfort level approaching a basic room at a lodge, and you will be able to stay wherever you end up that night. RVs can cost upward of $300 a night, so this flexibility does not come cheap. An internet search for RV or campervan rentals will get you started comparing costs versus benefits.

PROS: Combines your transportation, lodging, and meal prep into one space that goes where you go.

CONS: More expensive than driving a car and camping. Larger units will somewhat constrain campsite selection.

Fly, then drive a rental car

This may be your best option if you're coming a long way. With limited vacation time, you may not want to spend multiple days on both ends just getting to Yellowstone, and the added days also mean added hotel and fuel costs. The two closest major airports are in Salt Lake City, Utah, and Boise, Idaho. These may have better airfare prices than regional airports, but they will involve about five or six hours, respectively, of driving to actually reach the park. There are also smaller airports closer to the park. (See "Airports That Serve Yellowstone" later in this chapter.)

PROS: Flying can maximize vacation time spent in the park.

CONS: The expense of airfare and the limitations placed on baggage and what you can bring with you.

SUGGESTED ITINERARIES

Planning an itinerary for Yellowstone can be tough. You have things you want to see, but where are they? Where is the closest lodging? How far is it to the next thing on your list?

This section is designed to help you with that task. Like the rest of this book, it is organized by region so you can minimize driving and make the most of your time. Each section tells you how long to spend in each region, what lodging options are available in that region, and which must-see attractions are found there. And if you still have time, there's a list of additional suggested activities.

Rather than saying "Day One, Day Two," and so on, we simply state how long you should spend in each region. This way you can change the order of the days in your itinerary depending on which entrance you are using to enter and leave the park. We also did our best to suggest a minimum time for each activity, but the time you actually spend will depend a great deal on your personal interest levels and preferences. So with that said, let's go ahead and get planning!

Three-Day Itinerary

Three days is about the minimum time that we and other sources recommend to really see the best of what the park has to offer. If you have less time, simply choose the one or two days with the activities that most interest you and leave the other stuff for your next visit. Most likely, you will want to spend at least some of your time in the Geyser Region.

Geyser Region: 1 day

Must-See Attractions
Norris Geyser Basin: 1.5 hours
Midway Geyser Basin and Grand Prismatic Spring: 1 hour
Old Faithful and the Upper Geyser Basin: 2 or more hours
Fountain Paint Pots: 1 hour

Lodging Options
Geyser Region campgrounds: Norris, Madison
Geyser Region lodging: Old Faithful Inn, Old Faithful Snow Lodge and Cabins, Old Faithful Lodge Cabins

Several smaller geyser basins in this region also have impressive thermal features. Some of the best ones require a moderate day hike, so if you're up for that, it's a good place to stretch your legs. Details on these and additional activities where you can spend any extra time are under the Geyser Region in the Yellowstone Adventures by Region chapter. For more specific details on what all the different geyser basins have to offer, check out the Guide to the Geysers section.

Mammoth and Tower Regions: 1 day

Must-See Attractions
>Mammoth Hot Springs: 2 or more hours
>Tower Falls: 45 minutes
>Lamar Valley: 1–2 hours
>Petrified Tree: 30–45 minutes

Lodging Options
>Mammoth Region campgrounds: Mammoth, Indian Creek
>Tower Region campgrounds: Tower Fall, Slough Creek, Pebble Creek
>Mammoth Region lodging: Mammoth Hot Springs Hotel and Cabins
>Tower Region lodging: Roosevelt Lodge Cabins

There are many hiking and horseback riding opportunities in this region. In addition, this area is known for its abundant wildlife, so leave time for stopping and snapping photos. See other suggested activities in our Yellowstone Adventures sections for the Tower and Mammoth Regions.

For your best chance at spotting wildlife, try to visit the Lamar Valley early in the morning. Also in this region is the Blacktail Plateau Drive, a narrow, twisting, one-way dirt road that takes at least 35 minutes to drive and is closed to RVs and trailers. It can be a decent place to see deer and other wildlife, but the views from the main Grand Loop Road in this section are better.

Lake and Canyon Regions: 1 day

Must-See Attractions
>Grand Canyon of the Yellowstone: 2 or more hours

Wolves and bison are only one part of Yellowstone's exciting ecosystem.

Mud Volcano: 30–45 minutes
Hayden Valley: 30 minutes–1 hour
Yellowstone Lake and Fishing Bridge: 1 hour
West Thumb Geyser Basin: 1 hour
If you have more time, you can find lists of other activities to do in these regions in our Yellowstone Adventures sections for the Lake and Canyon regions.

Lodging Options
Lake Region campgrounds: Lewis Lake, Grant Village, Bridge Bay, and Fishing Bridge (RV only)
Canyon Region campgrounds: Canyon Village
Lake Region lodging: Grant Village, Lake Yellowstone Hotel and Cabins, Lake Lodge Cabins
Canyon Region lodging: Canyon Lodge and Cabins (includes both Dunraven and Cascade lodges)

If you come in from the South Entrance, stop first at the West Thumb Geyser Basin. If you come in from the East Entrance, you can leave this for later in your trip as you return from Old Faithful. Driving in from either entrance will give you good views of Yellowstone Lake and the chance to see Fishing Bridge and the visitor center near the lake. The visitor center is on the East Entrance Road, but it is only 0.7 mile from the intersection with the Grand Loop Road you will come in on from the South Entrance.

Five-Day Itinerary

If you plan to take a week off from work for your vacation, you can experience more of what Yellowstone has to offer. You will likely travel on the bookend weekends and have a full five days in the park, and this will give you ample time to enjoy yourself at a relaxing pace. Here are some ideas on how to spend those five days. Remember, you will probably need to switch the order around depending on how you're entering and leaving the park.

Geyser Region: 2 days

Must-See Attractions

Norris Geyser Basin: 2 hours
Midway Geyser Basin and Grand Prismatic Spring: 1 hour
Old Faithful and the Upper Geyser Basin: 3 or more hours
Fountain Paint Pots: 1 hour
Fairy Falls and Imperial Geyser (for hikers): Half a day
Biscuit Basin: 1 hour
Black Sand Basin: 1 hour

Lodging Options

Geyser Region campgrounds: Norris, Madison
Geyser Region lodging: Old Faithful Inn, Old Faithful Snow Lodge and Cabins, Old Faithful Lodge Cabins

This region offers the best opportunities for overnight backpacking trips as well as several excellent options for day hikes. You can also spend plenty of time at the Old Faithful area with all the various amenities there. More ideas for activities in this region are in the Geyser Region of the Yellowstone Adventures chapter. For more details on what all the different geyser basins have to offer, check out the Guide to the Geysers section.

AIRPORTS THAT SERVE YELLOWSTONE

Yellowstone is in the northwest corner of Wyoming, so it's not close to any large metropolitan areas with major airports. However, five small regional airports are within an hour or two of an entrance, although you might pay a little more for tickets.

Boise Airport (BOI) is about 350 miles, or about a six-hour drive, from the West Entrance to Yellowstone. You could also travel about the same time and distance to beautiful Grand Teton National Park, from which you can access the South Entrance to Yellowstone (see the Grand Teton sidebar to make the most of your visit). Make a loop of it as you come and go so you can see both parks.

From Salt Lake City International Airport (SLC) to the South Entrance, it's 339 miles and about six hours of driving through some beautiful areas, including Grand Teton National Park.

Smaller airports are closer to the park. Jackson Hole Airport (JAC) is just 50 miles from the South Entrance, and you'd get to experience Grand Teton on the way. Cody offers Yellowstone Regional Airport (COD), which is only 27 miles from the East Entrance. From Montana, the Bozeman Yellowstone International Airport (BZN) is just 90 miles from the North Entrance. Billings Logan International (BIL) is 67 miles from the Northeast Entrance, and the town of West Yellowstone has a small airport called Yellowstone Airport (WYS) that is serviced via Salt Lake International from June to early September. Idaho Falls Regional Airport (IDA) is 100 miles from the West Entrance.

There are signs in almost every building around Old Faithful telling you when the next eruption will happen, so find this out when you get there and then plan your time accordingly, as the Visitor Education Center and massive log structures are also worth seeing.

Mammoth Region: 1 day

Must-See Attractions

Mammoth Hot Springs: 2 or more hours
Boiling River: 2 hours

Lodging Options

Mammoth Region campgrounds: Mammoth, Indian Creek
Mammoth Region lodging: Mammoth Hot Springs Hotel and Cabins

Tower Falls offers scenery and, if you're lucky, a bighorn sheep sighting.

The Grand Canyon of the Yellowstone is an absolute must-see!

There are a lot of things to see at Mammoth regarding the history of the park, and there are some good shorter hikes in the area. A good place to raft is just outside the park in Gardiner, Montana. You'll find lists of suggested activities in our Yellowstone Adventures chapter under the Mammoth Region.

The lawns surrounding the hotel, visitor center, and historic Fort Yellowstone are the most likely places in the park to see elk. Change into your swimsuits before driving to the Boiling River; a vault toilet serves as the only changing area there.

Tower Region: 1 day

Must-See Attractions
    Tower Falls: 45 minutes
    Lamar Valley: 1–2 hours
    Petrified Tree: 30–45 minutes

Lodging Options

Tower Region campgrounds: Tower Fall, Slough Creek, Pebble Creek
Tower Region lodging: Roosevelt Lodge Cabins

There are many hiking and horseback riding opportunities in this region. In addition, this area is known for its abundant wildlife, so leave time for stopping and snapping photos. See other suggested activities in the Yellowstone Adventures chapter for the Tower and Mammoth Regions.

For your best chance at spotting wildlife, try to visit the Lamar Valley early in the morning. Also in this region is the Blacktail Plateau Drive, a narrow, twisting, one-way dirt road that takes at least 35 minutes to drive and is closed to RVs and trailers. It can be a decent place to see deer and other wildlife, but the views from the main Grand Loop Road in this section are better.

Lake and Canyon Regions: 1 day

Must-See Attractions

Grand Canyon of the Yellowstone: 2 or more hours
Mud Volcano: 30–45 minutes
Hayden Valley: 30 minutes–1 hour
Yellowstone Lake and Fishing Bridge: 1 hour
West Thumb Geyser Basin: 1 hour
Lists of other activities to do in these regions are in the Yellowstone Adventures sections for the Lake and Canyon regions.

Lodging Options

Lake Region campgrounds: Lewis Lake, Grant Village, Bridge Bay, and Fishing Bridge (RV only)
Canyon Region campgrounds: Canyon Village
Lake Region lodging: Grant Village, Lake Yellowstone Hotel and Cabins, Lake Lodge Cabins
Canyon Region lodging: Canyon Lodge and Cabins (includes both Dunraven and Cascade lodges)

If you come in from the South Entrance, stop first at the West Thumb Geyser Basin. If you come in from the East Entrance, you can leave this for later in your trip as you return from Old Faithful. Driving in from either entrance will give you good views of Yellowstone Lake and the chance to see Fishing Bridge and the visitor center there. The visitor center is on the East Entrance Road, but it is only 0.7 mile from the intersection with the Grand Loop Road you will use to drive from the South Entrance.

Seven Days and Beyond

If you have the opportunity to be in Yellowstone for a week or more, then we say "good for you!" Our last trip to the park was ten days and we enjoyed every minute of it. (We were, admittedly, a little tired after trying to fit in so many activities to prepare for writing this book!)

In essence, any itinerary beyond five days will look like the five-day itinerary in terms of regions visited, but there will be more time to fully explore all that each region has to offer. Search for activities in the Yellowstone Adventures sections that interest you the most and spend the extra time in those regions to fit it all in.

For example, you can take the time to do one or more of the hikes in each area, or you could add in an overnight backpacking trip for a true backcountry experience. In the Lake Region, you may want to go on a lake tour on a commercial boat, or you could rent a kayak or hire a guide and sea-kayak your way to one of the many campsites lining the southern shores of Yellowstone Lake. For more adventure, a canoe or kayak trip from Lewis Lake to Shoshone Lake awaits those with a little more experience on the water.

If you enjoy fly fishing, there are many miles of streams to tempt you, but you may have to stretch your legs a bit if you want to leave the crowds behind, as almost every mile of stream that borders a road will bring plenty of competition.

Settle down on a bench with a view to savor the Yellowstone experience.

Additional time beyond five days will allow you to not only see all of the main attractions but also get off the beaten path and experience some real adventure. Take advantage of that and create memories that will last a lifetime! So there you go; however long—or short—a time you have, it will be well spent in Yellowstone. We have always found that planning the trip is a big part of the fun of traveling, so read on and get started dreaming about your vacation!

ADDING ADVENTURE TO YOUR YELLOWSTONE TRIP

The suggestions we have listed for each region fall into these four basic categories. Here are some overviews of what each has to offer.

Hiking

This is the most common type of adventure in the park; there are literally hundreds of miles of trails available, although most of these are in the backcountry and not ideal for kids. If you are going for a hike, make sure you go prepared. Take a look at our Day Hiking Checklist for what you should bring as well as other hints and suggestions. To help you choose specific hikes, we have included detailed hike descriptions of those we feel are best suited to children, organized by region.

Each description starts with a quick overview to get you started. Distance, starting point, and GPS are pretty self-explanatory, although we didn't include GPS coordinates for trailheads that are already very easy to find. Some of the other details are a little more subjective. We consider several hundred feet of elevation gain per mile to be moderate; less than that is easy and more would count as difficult. In reality, rather than hard and fast rules and numbers, it was really based more on how we felt when we were actually hiking the trail with our kids. The times listed are based on our own experiences with our active children, aged eight to twelve (with baby in a backpack!), and don't include the time spent playing once we reached the main attraction. Our times tend to be toward the shorter end of the spectrum because our kids have abundant energy; use the times given as guidelines and adapt to your own kids' levels of energy and interest.

The hike to Trout Lake offers some fine vistas.

Bicycling

The park has limited opportunities for biking, but they do exist and there are some nice options. We recommend avoiding road biking, as the roads are narrow and congested with little to no shoulder, RVs have wide mirrors, people swerve as they view the scenery, and it's typically 20–30 miles between developed areas—not ideal conditions for kids. But there are a few places to cycle where motorized vehicles cannot go, and you can rent bikes at Old Faithful Snow Lodge if you're interested. The best options are reviewed in the appropriate sections below.

Horseback Riding

Horseback riding is available in the Canyon, Tower-Roosevelt, and Mammoth Hot Springs regions. These are typically one- to two-hour rides, but Tower-Roosevelt also hosts a wagon ride to an outdoor cookout. All these options are offered through Xanterra Parks & Resorts, which runs concessions in the park. More information is available on their website.

Getting on the Water

Motorized boating is only allowed on two of the larger lakes, Yellowstone Lake and Lewis Lake. These offer both scenic cruises and fishing options. There are options for canoeing and kayaking on these lakes, as well as one unique opportunity to canoe on Lewis Lake to a river that connects it with Shoshone Lake. Xanterra rents boats at the Bridge Bay Marina on Yellowstone Lake, and numerous guides and outfitters offer a wide variety of excursions that can be easily searched for online. Finally, rafting is not allowed in the park, but there are some good options in Gardiner, Montana, and Jackson Hole, Wyoming. If you do a little searching online you will find plenty of options. The Fishing and Boating section in the Best Bets chapter has more details on boating in Yellowstone.

BEST BETS

If you take the time and effort to visit Yellowstone, there are a few things you really owe it to yourself to see in order to get the most of your experience. We thought about our favorite attractions at Yellowstone and compared our notes with a number of other sources' "Best of Yellowstone" suggestions to compile this list. We sorted each feature by region to make your planning easier.

GEYSER REGION

Geysers are one of the quintessential experiences of Yellowstone, and while various types of geothermal features can be found in every region of the park, Geyser has the greatest number and variety of these amazing natural attractions.

Old Faithful

The most iconic landmark in Yellowstone is the Old Faithful Geyser, and it's definitely worth seeing. Its name suggests the reliability of its eruptions, which used to happen like clockwork. These days it's not quite so reliable, but rangers have devised a method of prediction, based on the duration of the previous eruption, that gives accuracy to within 15 minutes, which is still pretty great. Basically, if the eruption is less than two and a half minutes, the next eruption will happen in about 65 minutes. If the eruption lasts longer, the next eruption will happen in about 91 minutes.

The best approach is to head to the Old Faithful area at a time that works for your schedule and expect to spend at least 90 minutes there. The good news is that there are plenty of other things to do while you wait. You can visit the Old Faithful

If there's one feature everyone knows, it's Old Faithful.

Grand Prismatic Spring really needs to be seen to be believed.

Inn, the largest log structure in the world. You can visit the Old Faithful Visitor Education Center, which has nice, very informative displays about every aspect of the park. You can grab a bite to eat at any number of venues or bring a picnic. The Yellowstone Park Foundation also has a great display of old photos of the park and informative kiosks that explain some of the work it does on the park's behalf. This is also a great time for kids to work on their Junior Ranger booklets.

Finally, remember that Old Faithful is just one of many features in the Upper Geyser Basin, so why not use your time to walk the trails and boardwalks and visit other impressive examples of geysers? Suffice it to say you don't need to be bored as you wait for the next eruption, and chalkboard signs all around inform you of when that will happen, give or take 15 minutes.

Midway Geyser Basin and Grand Prismatic Spring

Midway Geyser Basin features two amazing hot springs. The first you will see is Excelsior Geyser, which pumps an amazing 4000 gallons of hot water per minute into the Firehole River.

Norris Geyser Basin includes the tallest geyser in the world.

The second you come to is Grand Prismatic Spring, the most colorful spring in Yellowstone and the largest in diameter. This has been a must-see every time we've visited the park; it's simply stunning and unlike anything else you will see. The spring looks like a window right into the center of the earth, with richer, cooler colors in the warmest and deepest central portions of the pool. As the water flows onto the surrounding terrain, it cools in the shallower areas and hydrophilic bacteria create a carpet of warmer reds, oranges, and yellows. It is simply otherworldly, and if you've only seen pictures of it you will wonder if they have been manipulated until you see it for yourself. If you want the bird's-eye view favored by photographers, check out our description of the Fairy Falls hike to learn how to get to that vantage point.

Norris Geyser Basin

Norris Geyser Basin is the oldest and hottest basin in the park, and it includes the tallest geyser in the world. Don't hold your breath, however: unfortunately Steamboat Geyser only erupts a few times a decade! Don't let this deter you, because there are dozens of other features to see in this large and diverse basin as well as a museum that provides a good education on what makes geothermal features function the way that they do. There are two main parts to Norris: Porcelain Basin, viewed via a short walk; and Back Basin, which has a boardwalk-and-trail loop of roughly a mile depending on which routes you take. Many of the geysers in this basin may be average in size, but they are also very active. If you spend some time here, you are bound to see at least one geyser doing its thing, which will delight your kids.

MAMMOTH REGION

Found in the northwest portion of the park, this region offers a number of interesting places to visit, but none are more remarkable than its namesake, Mammoth Hot Springs.

Mammoth Hot Springs makes a great place to pose for family photos.

Mammoth Hot Springs

There are other hot springs that create terraces as they flow, but none are so large, diverse, or simply magnificent as those at Mammoth Hot Springs. If you approach this area from the east, you can actually see the white shapes of the springs from miles away. And each time you visit, the springs are going to look different because the water is constantly changing its location, volume, flow, and direction such that this landscape is as dynamic as it is unique. This area of the park is the only one open year-round, and it has always served as park headquarters, so it's rather developed. In addition to the springs, there is a lot of history here for those who are interested, as well as a near guarantee of seeing elk walking among the buildings.

Tower Falls has been attracting photographers since at least 1931. (USGS photo)

TOWER REGION

This region in the northeast corner of the park is best known for its abundant wildlife viewing opportunities.

Tower Falls

Tower Falls is this area's namesake feature, and it's worth a visit. The falls themselves drop 132 feet and create such a mist as they strike the bottom that you can often see a rainbow. But an additional unique feature of this area is the canyon from which the river drops, as the rocks there have eroded into columns and pinnacles (or towers) of all manner of shape and size. In fact, Thomas Moran's painting of this striking geologic

The Tower Region is a good spot for finding bison.

feature was instrumental in convincing Congress to grant approval for this first of America's national parks.

Lamar Valley

The Lamar Valley is synonymous with wildlife, and as you drive from Tower Junction through this valley toward the Northeast Entrance, you will pass through the territory of two distinct wolf packs. They are here because the game is here, and you will almost certainly see bison along this stretch of road. The narrowness of the river bottom before you actually reach the Lamar Valley tends to bring them closer to your car than in other areas. Pronghorn antelope abound here, and elk and sandhill crane sightings are also common. Go early or late in the day to increase your chances of seeing abundant wildlife.

CANYON REGION

Canyon offers visitors some excellent wildlife-viewing opportunities in the Hayden Valley, but the most spectacular feature in

All the water plunging over the Lower Falls of the Yellowstone sprays dramatic mist into the canyon.

arguably the entire park is located here: the Grand Canyon of the Yellowstone River.

Grand Canyon of the Yellowstone, Upper and Lower Falls

The colorful walls of the Grand Canyon of the Yellowstone are the source of the park's name, and this amazing area is another must-see. There are two waterfalls here; Upper Falls, a short distance upstream of the deep canyon, is beautiful, but Lower Falls is the one that plunges 308 feet at the beginning of the massive gash in the earth known as the Grand Canyon of the Yellowstone. By itself that would be startling enough to warrant a look, but for miles downstream a variety of minerals color the canyon walls, creating a delightful palette of yellow, orange, pink, and cream, which stands in beautiful contrast to the harder gray stone and the green trees that live in the canyon. More than a dozen vantage points are accessible from different portions of North and South Rim drives, and all are beautiful. In fact, a photographer could spend all day here getting different shots as the sun progressively highlights new portions of the canyon. Make sure this area is on your itinerary.

Hayden Valley

If you are visiting the Grand Canyon of the Yellowstone (as you should!), you will probably pass through Hayden Valley either coming or going. This broad valley is very scenic, and the Yellowstone River flows along the eastern side as it makes its journey to the canyon. Ducks and geese are always present on this section of river, sometimes with stately swans; you can also frequently see pelicans with their massive, fish-catching bill. This is also a great spot to see bison and possibly even the wolf pack that calls this region home. There are numerous pullouts for viewing wildlife and taking the pictures that will be your mementos of the park.

LAKE REGION

Yellowstone Lake is a huge expanse of water that now fills what was once the caldera of a massive volcano. The lake is deep, cold, blue, and beautiful; you won't want to miss it.

Hayden Valley's abundance of water and grazing areas makes for great wild-life viewing.

Yellowstone Lake

Yellowstone Lake covers 132 square miles, making it the largest lake in North America higher than 7000 feet in elevation. It is also home to the largest inland population of cutthroat trout anywhere, which has always confounded biologists because these fish are historically only found in waterways that drain into the Pacific. The lake certainly does not, but speculation is that it may have at one time. The Fishing Bridge Visitor Center can share these and many other fascinating facts about this massive body of water. And while fishing is no longer allowed on Fishing Bridge, it is still a great place to view the cutthroat trout—so named because of the red color on their gill covers—as they spawn in June and early July.

Yellowstone Lake (NPS photo)

West Thumb Geyser Basin

This basin is a bit smaller than those in the Geyser Region, but it has a few unusual features, and its location right on the shores of Yellowstone Lake makes it special. One hot spring here is named Abyss Pool because of its great depth, which also gives it a nice blue coloration. Another somewhat humorous feature is the Fishing Cone, a hot spring that lies right at the water's edge where early visitors dipped freshly caught fish to cook them on the spot. Only in Yellowstone!

There are your "Top 10" sights organized by region, but we want to encourage you to not leave it at that. There are many other geyser basins, waterfalls, historic places, and other attractions to see; so if you have the time, be sure to explore those as well.

More important, and as we stated before, we firmly believe that Yellowstone is a *wild* place, and to fully experience this you need to get off the roads, off the boardwalks, and into adventure. Get off the beaten path a bit and get a little dirty; get a little closer to nature; breathe it in. The Yellowstone Adventures By Region chapter has multiple suggestions, also organized by region, for just how to do that. We made sure to include something for everyone, at any level.

Fountain Paint Pot

GUIDE TO THE GEYSERS (AND OTHER ATTRACTIONS)

Yellowstone is special for a lot of reasons, but one thing that makes it particularly so is its abundance of geothermal activity. In fact, Yellowstone contains about half of the earth's geothermal features within its boundary, making it the best place in the world to see and learn about these natural wonders.

There are more than ten thousand thermal features in the park, including more than three hundred geysers. Other marvels include brilliantly colored hot springs, bubbling mudpots, and steaming fumaroles. A mudpot is simply a hot spring filled with boiling mud instead of hot water, and a fumarole is also called a steam vent. These features exist here due to a massive underlying magma body, the Yellowstone Caldera. The largest supervolcano in North America, it encompasses an area of 1350 square miles. It is the interaction of this tremendous heat source and the subterranean groundwater that creates the many hydrothermal wonders of Yellowstone National Park.

Considering the number of features in the park, you simply cannot see them all. The good news is that the park has made the most impressive attractions easy to access, and with even just a couple of days, you should have time to see the best of them. Use this section to help plan which to visit during your vacation.

GEYSER REGION

We named the southwest portion of the park the Geyser Region for a reason: it has the largest abundance of geothermal features in the park, by far.

The West Thumb Geyser Basin is well worth a visit.

Norris Geyser Basin

Starting from the north, the first geyser basin you come to is Norris, right at Norris Junction. This is an excellent choice for your first foray into geothermal features because a museum here explains the four different classes of features and the science behind what makes them work. Norris Geyser Basin is one of the most vast and thermally active basins in the park. It includes both acidic and alkaline waters, a wide variety of colors, and abundant hot springs and geysers. Its features are constantly changing.

There are actually two basins here. Porcelain Basin, next to the museum, is the smaller, and its water's silty blue appearance comes from the abundance of silica, the primary component in glass. The silica turns white when the water evaporates and rings the blue pools with white deposits, giving the entire basin a beautiful appearance and also giving rise to its name. The main boardwalk loop here is a mere half mile, and an auxiliary loop can add another half mile.

The second basin, Back Basin, is much larger, and its features are more spread out. Its trail is quite a bit longer, at 1.5 miles, but it takes you past many fascinating elements. Most famous is Steamboat Geyser, the tallest in the world at more than 300 feet! But you'll have to be quite lucky to see it erupt, as it is completely unpredictable and decades can pass between eruptions. To shorten the loop, take a shortcut just after passing this geyser.

Our boys were delighted by the numerous springs and active geysers just off the boardwalk. We spent several minutes watching Vixen Geyser erupt mere feet away, so close that we were a little afraid for the boys' safety. But the drops of overspray that hit us were either too cool or too small to bother them at all. There are about twenty different features on the larger loop, so you're bound to find at least a few along the path that will delight you and your kids.

Artists Paintpots

Heading south on the Grand Loop Road, the next attraction you come to is Artists Paintpots, just 3.7 miles from Norris Junction. This trail is a 1.1-mile lollipop that goes up a hillside with some nice views from the top. What's also interesting is that the features at the bottom of the hillside tend to collect more water and form hot-springs pools, while the water drains more rapidly from the upper features, rendering them mudpots. Sometimes these mudpots spurt blobs of mud several feet into the air before they plop back down into the warm gray slime. The boys thought that was pretty awesome.

This area has some cool mudpot features and a moderate and pleasant hike. But if you're pressed for time and can only visit one set of paint pots, we suggest you head a bit farther south to the more brilliantly colored Fountain Paint Pot.

Fountain Paint Pot and Firehole Lake Drive

As you head south from Madison Junction, the next hydro-thermal feature you come to is Fountain Paint Pot. A short half-mile boardwalk takes you past all four types of thermal features: geysers, hot springs, fumaroles, and mudpots. It is also a great place to see bacterial mats that thrive in the warm waters of hot-spring outflows. There are twelve different features on this short path, and the parking lot is immediately adjacent to the Grand Loop Road, which makes for quick and easy access. In addition, the far side of the boardwalk provides expansive views of the Lower Geyser Basin, better views than you get from Fountain Flat Drive. These factors combine to give you a lot of bang for your buck.

On the other side of the road from Fountain Paint Pot is Firehole Lake Drive. This one-way road goes in a counterclockwise direction; the entrance is 1.2 miles south from the Fountain parking lots. On this road you will drive for 2 miles and pass about five different features, all of which are interesting but not quite as spectacular as others within the park. Still, it's worth a look if you have twenty minutes to spare, although on a recent cold day none could entice our boys out of the car.

Midway Geyser Basin and Grand Prismatic Spring

Just to the south of Firehole Lake Drive is the turnoff to Midway Geyser Basin on the west side of the road. Take it! This basin contains two amazing sights, Grand Prismatic Spring and Excelsior Geyser. Grand Prismatic Spring is the largest and most colorful in the park, almost guaranteed to take your breath away. A boardwalk provides up-close views of the edge of this gem, but you can achieve even better views from above if you take the time to explore the first part of the Fairy Falls hike, details of which are in the Geyser Region section of the Yellowstone Adventures chapter. Grand Prismatic is the attraction that graces so many of the postcards and calendars you see, and it's something that you won't want to miss.

The other feature here, Excelsior Geyser, is now really more of a huge hot spring than a geyser. Nevertheless, it dumps thousands of gallons of water into the nearby Firehole River in another iconic Yellowstone scene that is well worth seeing.

Biscuit Basin

Part of the Upper Geyser Basin, this small basin contains about seven neat features including Sapphire Pool, Black Opal Pool, and Jewel Geyser. The boardwalk is a two-thirds-mile lollipop loop that first crosses the Firehole River. Additional hiking trails leave from the trailhead at the back side of the basin. Sapphire Pool alone is worth the quick stop if you can find the time.

Black Sand Basin

Another small basin within the larger Upper Geyser Basin, this area also boasts several jewel-like geysers and hot springs. Emerald Pool is a beautiful green, as its name implies, and it is ringed with yellows and oranges. Opalescent Pool formed more recently and flooded a stand of pine trees in the process, creating a stand of bleached trees surrounded by colorful waters. The trail to see these attractions is a mere 0.4 mile.

Upper Geyser Basin and Old Faithful

If you want to be sure to see a geyser erupt, then this is your place. Old Faithful is, of course, the most famous geyser in the park, but park rangers also predict the eruption times of four other geysers in this basin: Castle, Grand, Daisy, and Riverside. Old Faithful itself erupts 100–185 feet into the air every 60–110 minutes, and the rangers can predict the time to within about 15 minutes. In the meantime you will have plenty to do in the area, whether it's touring the visitor education center, shopping at gift stores, grabbing a quick bite to eat, or hiking the trails of the Upper Geyser Basin. Did we mention the other features? While they are overshadowed by their famous counterpart, there are more than thirty unique hydrothermal features in the entire basin.

MAMMOTH REGION

While lacking the number and variety of features found in the Geyser Region, the Mammoth Region is still a must-see due to its namesake, Mammoth Hot Springs.

Mammoth Hot Springs is a massive deposit of travertine that can be seen from miles away; in fact, it is one of the world's best examples of a travertine-depositing hot spring. Another fascinating aspect of this spring is that the location and direction of the water flows are constantly changing. Most of the hot spring consists of dry travertine deposits from previous years, while a smaller portion is actually active and growing. The locations of the actively growing areas change from year to year so each visit is different. When people visit for a second or third time and find their favorite spots no longer look they same, they might wonder if the hot springs are drying up, but park scientists have determined that the overall volume of flow has remained quite constant from year to year; it is simply the distribution of the water that has changed.

The hot springs are composed of both upper and lower terraces. The lower terraces are reached via boardwalks served by parking areas adjacent to the green lawns of the Mammoth Hot Springs developed area. The upper terraces can be reached by hiking up from the lower ones, or you can reach them by taking a 2-mile drive south from the developed area on the Grand Loop Road toward Norris. Upper Terrace Drive is a scenic 1.5-mile, one-way loop that first takes you to the upper-level boardwalks and then winds through other interesting features that can easily be viewed from your car.

The hot springs will be readily apparent as you near the Mammoth Hot Springs Junction and the Albright Visitor Center; they should be considered a must-see when visiting the park.

TOWER REGION

We aren't saying this region has zero thermal features, but we will say they don't measure up to what the rest of the park has to offer. When you're here, focus on hiking and wildlife opportunities, and get your geothermal fix while visiting the other regions of the park.

Bison roam the Lamar Valley.

CANYON REGION

You visit this region to see the Grand Canyon of the Yellowstone and not necessarily thermal features. But there is one noteworthy exception.

The Mud Volcano Area—on the Grand Loop Road south of Canyon Junction, at the southern end of Hayden Valley and very close to LeHardy Rapids—is filled primarily with mudpots and fumaroles. It is one of the most acidic parts of the park, while many of the other features are more alkaline. The acidity breaks down rock into the small particles of silt that give rise to the abundant mud in most of the features here. But what makes this area really memorable is the pungent odor caused by hydrogen sulfide gas, which gives the entire area a rotten-egg smell that your kids will not soon forget!

Visiting this attraction doesn't take a lot of time. You can walk a two-thirds-mile boardwalk trail, and if you do it in the clockwise direction, it's less steep. For an even shorter stop, simply visit the two most impressive features, which are, fortunately, very near the parking lot. One is the Mud Volcano itself, which is now more of a cauldron, and the other is the Dragons Mouth Spring. The gases from this fumarole emerge from a cave in the hillside in a way that really captures the imagination.

LAKE REGION

This region has only one geothermal area, but it is still quite impressive and has a colorful past. West Thumb Geyser Basin is right on the shores of Yellowstone Lake just north of Grant Village, at the junction of the Grand Loop Road and the South Entrance Road. It includes the feature known as Fishing Cone, described in the Best Bets chapter. Seeing the features at West Thumb Geyser Basin requires only a short walk. An outer trail of half a mile and an inner loop of a mere quarter mile together will lead you past a variety of geothermal features including mudpots, hot springs, fumaroles, and even geysers, although the geysers in this area are no longer very active. Additionally, the geyser basin's location at the edge of the lake makes for some stunning views.

YELLOWSTONE WILDLIFE

Yellowstone has many wonderful things to see, including the wide variety of wildlife that calls this place home. With more than 67 different species, the park contains the largest concentration of mammals in the Lower 48 states; and more than 300 species of birds spend at least some part of their year here. This section will give you ideas on where to get started in your quest to see these amazing animals.

The first thing to keep in mind is that most wildlife is primarily active during the earliest and latest parts of the day. If you really want the best chance of seeing a lot of wildlife, make the

Both cow and bull bison sport horns. (NPS/Jim Peaco photo)

effort to get up early and head out at first light. Alternatively, having an early dinner and then spending the waning hours of daylight out in the field can dramatically improve your odds of seeing animals. Finally, it never hurts to bring along a few pairs of binoculars. We find that giving our kids their own binoculars, and sometimes even their own cameras, increases their enjoyment and the amount of time they will tolerate sitting around looking for wildlife. Remember the park's warnings about getting too close to wild animals. They may seem tame, but they are unpredictable.

BISON (BUFFALO). If you spend much time at all in Yellowstone, you are going to see bison. Many people call these animals buffalo, but the correct term is bison, since "buffalo" refers to species like water buffalo in Asia and Cape buffalo in Africa, species that are more similar to the domestic cow. This large ungulate can be found anywhere in the park, especially in grassy meadows and sage-studded flats where it can find enough forage to satisfy its ample appetite. But for your best odds of seeing a lot of bison, head to the northeastern portions of the park. The drive from Fishing Bridge to Tower Junction takes you through the Hayden Valley, a common place to spot these animals. Our favorite area, however, is along the drive from Tower Junction to the Northeast Entrance, particularly the first part of this road between the junction and Slough Creek Campground. Here the valley is narrower, which means the bison are typically closer to the road, making for better viewing and photo opportunities. As you continue east, you will come to the Lamar Valley, which is famous for its wildlife. But the valley is broad, and much of what you see will be farther from the road. Finally, the Grand Loop Road between Tower Junction and Mammoth Hot Springs is another very likely place to see these big beasts.

PRONGHORN ANTELOPE. This is another animal with a problematic name, as it's not really an antelope but more closely related to the goat family. Some locals actually call them speed goats, which is apt because they are the fastest land animals in North America. This also happens to be the only continent on which they are found. They are a true North American original! Speed and eyesight are their main defenses, so they tend to favor more open areas of sage and grassland. Their orange-and-white coats make them relatively easy to spot, and their graceful forms are a delight to watch when they move, and especially when they run. Because of the habitat they favor, pronghorn are found in many of the most likely places for bison as well. We always see them from the Northeast Entrance Road in the Lamar Valley and all the way to Tower Junction. The Grand Loop Road between Tower and Mammoth is also a likely spot to see these speedsters.

MULE DEER. Mule deer are so named because of their large ears (like a mule's), and although they are a bit larger than pronghorns, they are tougher to spot because their coats are better camouflage and they tend to stay in more wooded areas. But

Pronghorn are strikingly graceful.

Mule deer bucks

A bull elk bugling

there are a lot of deer in the park, and if you get out early and late in the day, you are likely to see a few. There also tend to be a few deer hanging around most campsites, since they have learned not to fear people and the human presence helps to keep the predators at bay. Deer are in every part of the park, so keep your eyes peeled.

ELK. When we first started visiting Yellowstone, there were 20,000 elk in the park, and spotting them was about as easy as spotting bison. Over the years, however, that number has dropped to about 4800, and sightings of these animals are not as common as they used to be. Another reason they can be tough to see is that in summer they favor the higher mountain meadows where the grass is greenest, and these can be far from the main routes of travel. But if you pay attention to where the grass meets the tree line at the edges of Yellowstone's many meadows, you still have a good chance of spotting one. And if you're looking for a sure thing, you can simply drive to Mammoth Hot Springs and look for them on the many green lawns in the complex. This may not seem as romantic as spotting one in its wilder environs, but an elk is still an elk, and they

A bighorn sheep ewe and her little lamb (NPS photo)

are beautiful no matter where they're found (And, speaking of romance, keep in mind that bulls are particularly dangerous during rutting season!). Other good places to spot elk are the Hayden Valley and along the Firehole and Gibbon rivers in the Madison area.

BIGHORN SHEEP. The most recent count, in 2015, put the population of sheep in the park at about 330. When you consider the size of the park, finding one of these iconic animals may seem like looking for a needle in a haystack. But since they mainly inhabit steep, high-alpine habitat, the amount of the park that is actually suitable for them is relatively small. Mount Everts sees the most concentrated use by sheep year-round, and they are often seen on hikes to the top of Mount Washburn and the Dunraven Pass area as well. A population of sheep utilizes the river canyon between Mammoth Hot Springs and the town of Gardiner, Montana. This band of sheep is especially visible during the winter but is always present in this area and can sometimes be seen along the road to the North Entrance. Another good

Watch for grazing moose in thickets. (NPS photo)

option is the cliffs along the Yellowstone River near Tower Falls and up to Tower–Roosevelt Junction. The sheep are found on either side of the river here, the opposite side being accessible via hikes up Specimen Ridge and from the Yellowstone River Picnic Area on the Northeast Entrance Road close to Tower–Roosevelt Junction.

MOOSE. The moose population in Yellowstone is quite small, currently estimated at fewer than two hundred animals, and since they often live in thickly wooded areas they can be very tough to see. In the summer they prefer wetland habitat and feed on soft and nutritious aquatic plants on lake bottoms, typically dipping their heads under water for extended periods to feed. They also commonly browse willow bushes along stream sides. Look for them any place where forest meets water, especially marshy lakes and willow-lined streams. The most common place to find them is in the southwest portion of the park—the Shoshone Lake and Lewis River system, for example—which is also very difficult to access. Other areas include Soda Butte Creek, Pelican Creek, and the Gallatin River drainages.

If you really have your heart set on seeing a moose, you should consider spending time in Grand Teton National Park, immediately to the south of Yellowstone. The abundant lakes and rivers of this park make for better moose habitat, and sightings there are much more common. Grand Teton even has a "Moose District" at its southern end. Moose frequent the areas around Jackson Lake Lodge and Oxbow Bend, and many people recommend driving the Moose–Wilson Road. Be out right at sunup or sundown for the best chance of seeing one of these elusive animals—and keep your eyes on the willows.

BEARS. There are two species of bear in Yellowstone, black bears and grizzly bears, and both can be found throughout the park. Because the grizzly is on the US endangered species list (though it's expected to be removed from the list soon due to the success of efforts to revive the population), many policies guiding its management affect how you can use the park. The most obvious

Spotting a grizzly bear is guaranteed to get your heart racing. (NPS/Neal Herbert photo)

Seeing an alpha wolf like this one is an exciting prospect. (NPS/Neal Herbert photo)

of these are the bear management areas where human access is limited at certain times of the year. You can learn more about grizzly bears in Yellowstone on the park website.

In general, if you're out and about with kids, you're probably going to want to *minimize* your chance of seeing a bear, not maximize it. And really, there is no sure way to see bears; it will be more a matter of luck. But there are still opportunities to see bears safely. The first is simply to stay in your car and go to areas where you can spot game at long distances, such as the Lamar Valley, at peak times of day. The Tower Falls area also seems to have better-than-average bear sightings.

Have you ever wondered how certain containers are certified "grizzly proof"? Well, at the Grizzly & Wolf Discovery Center, our second suggested option, you can meet the bear that does the testing. Just head one block out of the park's West Entrance to find the discovery center. Yes, this is a zoo, but it's really more than that, with the animals in fairly natural habitat. It's very well managed and works in conjunction with the park. It isn't quite the same as seeing one in the wild, but it's probably safer and is an engaging place for kids to see wildlife you are not likely to find otherwise.

WOLVES. Spotting wolves in Yellowstone is another quest that will likely depend on luck unless you become dedicated to the prospect, as a number of people do. You will recognize those people when you see a cluster of them and their vehicles somewhere along the road, with a bunch of conservation-related stickers on their cars and an impressive display of massive binoculars, spotting scopes, and cameras mounted on tripods and all pointing the same direction. Wolves have engendered an almost cult-like following, and you will probably recognize their followers when you see them.

One morning Harley left the family at camp at first light and drove out with his binoculars to the Lamar Valley, hoping to see wildlife. He spotted the usual animals you expect to see but not the grizzly or wolf he wanted, so he started back to camp for breakfast. But as he passed the turnoff to Slough Creek Campground, he noticed a scene like the one described above, so he pulled over. Sure enough, there was a den in a grove of aspen trees a mile or so west of the turnoff, and a particular black wolf had been seen regularly in the area. He grabbed his best binoculars and walked over to the small rise where everyone was set up, and soon someone called out that they'd spotted a wolf. They graciously allowed others to look through their spotting scope, and once Harley knew the wolf's location, he set up his binoculars on a tripod and allowed others to watch the animal through his lenses. That made for a pretty cool morning!

This sort of solitude isn't common on Yellowstone Lake these days! (NPS/Ed Bovy photo)

To see wolves, the Lamar Valley and Slough Creek areas are good bets, as is the Hayden Valley, where the Canyon pack has a rendezvous site visible from the Grizzly Overlook. This overlook is simply the first pullout south of Alum Creek along the Grand Loop Road, so named because there used to be an interpretive sign there about why the surrounding habitat was excellent for grizzly bears. Packs use all these areas, but the wolves' number and distribution change annually. If you are really serious, some online searching will reveal reams of information, and you can even sign up for daily updates via email newsletters and the like.

Finally, as with the grizzly, if you really want to see a wolf, you can head just outside the West Entrance to the Grizzly & Wolf Discovery Center. None of the individual animals here could survive in the wild, and the Center provides people with a chance to see these interesting species up close.

OTHER PREDATORS (MOUNTAIN LION, BOBCAT, FOX, COYOTE). All of these animals are present in the park, but it's quite rare to see any except the coyote. Seeing a mountain lion is a one-in-a-million proposition, as their territories are huge and they are very secretive. Bobcats are not as wily, but they are still pretty elusive, and it's a special treat to see one. Red foxes are a bit more common but still unusual, while coyotes are larger and more visible and tend to favor more open areas. The wildlife-rich and more open northern portions of the park are your best bet to spot foxes and coyotes.

FISHING AND BOATING

Children have a natural fascination for things involving water, and in this section we provide some guidelines for enjoying fishing and boating activities in Yellowstone.

Fishing

Fishing is a time-honored tradition in the park and one of the major attractions for legions of anglers who hope to catch one of the famed Yellowstone cutthroat trout. But this is not necessarily a great place to introduce kids to fishing, as fishing here typically means fly fishing in fast-moving streams, casting to trout that have seen fishermen before. However, some lakes can be reached with a little hiking effort that may leave some of the crowds behind. If you want to fish in the park, you need to buy a fishing permit, which is available at any visitor center, ranger station, or general store in the park. Permits are available for three- or seven-day periods, or you can get an annual license. Kids under sixteen can fish for free if they are under direct supervision of an adult permit holder or have a responsible adult sign a form. The regulations are complicated and well beyond the scope of this book, so be sure to stop in at a visitor center to get the park's fishing booklet and ask for advice on where to go.

Numerous guides are licensed to offer services in the park, and lists of these can be found in neighboring towns' chambers of commerce or more easily with a basic internet search. Xanterra (see Resources) also provides chartered fishing excursions on Yellowstone Lake or full-day guided fly-fishing excursions. These can be pricey, depending on how many people are in your group; you can also rent equipment for an additional fee. You must still purchase a valid fishing permit from the park.

Boating

Power boating is allowed on most of Yellowstone Lake and on Lewis Lake, but all other lakes allow only nonmotorized boating. The only river open to boating of any kind is the Lewis River Channel that connects Lewis and Shoshone lakes in the southwest portion of the park.

Whether you bring a massive powerboat or a simple float tube, you will need to buy a permit and your craft will be inspected for invasive aquatic species. Permits can be obtained at the South Entrance, the Grant Village backcountry office, and the Bridge Bay Ranger Station. Permits specifically for nonmotorized craft can also be purchased at the Mammoth backcountry office. If all you need is a simple float-tube permit, you can obtain one at the Northeast Entrance, the Canyon and Old Faithful backcountry offices, the Lewis Lake Campground, and the Bechler Ranger Station (on the park's western border).

If you would rather not bring your own boat but still want to get out on the water, Xanterra will rent you an outboard or a rowboat at the Bridge Bay Marina on Yellowstone Lake. These boats are available on a first come, first served basis.

CANOE OR KAYAK ADVENTURE ON THE LEWIS RIVER CHANNEL. As mentioned above, only one waterway in Yellowstone is open to boating, the Lewis River Channel. It connects Lewis Lake to Shoshone Lake, which lies in a primitive area only accessible this way or by a fairly long hike. We have never done this trip, but it's on our bucket list. A quick internet search will turn up multiple guide and outfitting services that can lead you on this trip, or, if you have the skill and experience, you can tackle it on your own. If you do go on this trip, please tell us about it!

SEA KAYAKING ON YELLOWSTONE LAKE. Another way to get more time on the water is to take a kayak trip on the southern shores of Yellowstone Lake. Most of the lake's southern arms and bays are closed to motorized traffic, so they offer solitude and a true backcountry experience without having to walk a long way, although you will have to paddle! There are also a large number of campsites along the shore that can be reserved through the backcountry office, just like backpacking sites. Once again, a quick internet search will turn up numerous outfitters happy to lead you on your trip, while if you have the tools and know-how you can tackle this on your own. Bring your fishing rod and license!

GRAND TETON NATIONAL PARK

Grand Teton, another iconic national park, lies within easy striking distance of Yellowstone, so why not plan a little time to visit it since you're already in the area? Making a trip to Grand Teton can be as simple as planning your travel itinerary to either enter or leave Yellowstone via the South Entrance—since that will mean driving through Grand Teton. As with most parks, the subjects of many of the area's famous images can be found at roadside pullouts and designated parking areas, so even those who don't stray far from the car can still have a great experience. We always advocate actually getting your kids out of the car and off the asphalt, but if you're simply driving through Grand Teton on your way in or out of Yellowstone, you can still take just a little extra time and see some wonderful sights.

Grand Teton is a much smaller park than Yellowstone. It is only a one-hour drive from Yellowstone's South Entrance to the southern end of Grand Teton if you stay on the main roads—and the main roads get you plenty of great views. You will need to pay a separate $30 entrance fee unless you already have an annual pass, but that is pretty cheap for all you can see in even one day.

TOP SIGHTS

The four best-known views in Grand Teton are Oxbow Bend, the Snake River Overlook, Schwabacher Landing, and the Mormon Row barns. All of these except for the last are reachable via turnouts or short access roads right along the main north–south highway through the park, US Highway 89/191. Even the historic old barns are less than five minutes off this route.

Let's assume you're coming into Grand Teton from the north as a day trip from Yellowstone. The first thing you should do is stop in at the Colter Bay Visitor Center if you want to get your national park passport book stamped, talk to rangers, investigate day-hiking options, and learn more about the park. This visitor center has all services, and

Snake River Overlook

some nice picnic areas along Jackson Lake here offer wonderful views of the Teton Range.

Continuing south, you will pass the Jackson Lake Lodge area before coming to Jackson Lake Junction. Here, you want to stay on US 89/191 toward Moran Junction; don't take the turn onto Teton Park Road. Shortly past the junction, you will come to the Oxbow Bend turnout, and this is your first stop of the big four. The broad, slow-moving oxbow of the Snake River can be a good place to spot moose.

From the oxbow, continue south on US 89/191 toward Moran Junction. At the junction, turn right to stay on this highway toward Jackson Hole. From this junction, you will drive 10 miles through the relatively flat, broad expanse of Elk Ranch Flats, then start gaining elevation as you leave the flats for a bench overlooking the Snake River, with the Grand Tetons as the backdrop. This is the famed Snake River Overlook, where Ansel Adams stood when he took one of his most famous images.

From the overlook, continue driving almost 5 miles south and watch for signs for Schwabacher Landing. This short spur road to the west will take you to yet another spot with the Snake River in front and the

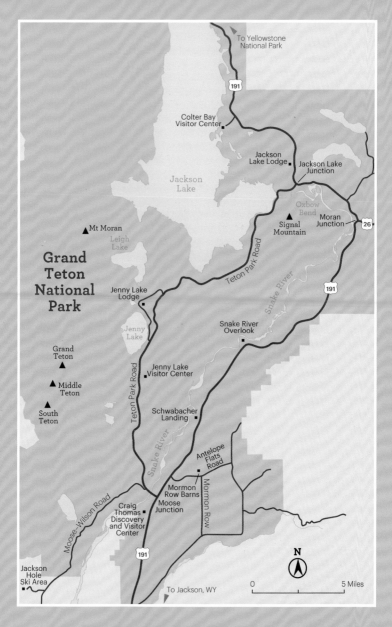

To Yellowstone
National Park

191

Colter Bay
Visitor Center

Jackson
Lake Lodge

Jackson Lake
Junction

Jackson
Lake

Oxbow
Bend

Moran
Junction

26

Signal
Mountain

Mt Moran

Leigh
Lake

Teton Park Road

Snake River

191

**Grand
Teton
National
Park**

Jenny Lake
Lodge

Jenny
Lake

Snake River
Overlook

Grand
Teton

Teton Park Road

Middle
Teton

Jenny Lake
Visitor Center

South
Teton

Schwabacher
Landing

Snake River

Antelope
Flats
Road

Mormon
Row Barns

Mormon Row

Moose
Junction

Moose-Wilson Road

Craig
Thomas
Discovery
and Visitor
Center

191

Jackson
Hole
Ski Area

To Jackson, WY

N

0   5 Miles

Teton Range in the back, but you are closer to the river now, and multiple viewing points of the mountains provide interesting perspectives.

Once you leave the landing and rejoin US 89/191, continue south for 2.7 miles and then turn left (east) on Antelope Flats Road. Follow this road approximately 1.5 miles and you will see a cluster of historic old barns and homesteads to the north, near the intersection with the Mormon Row Road. It almost seems as if they were placed here specifically to create photo opportunities.

From this point you have two options, depending on the time you have. The quickest way back to Yellowstone is to simply head back to

Mormon Row Barns

Oxbow Bend in fall

the highway, turn north, and retrace your route. If you have more time, the park headquarters is less than 2 miles away to the south in Moose, Wyoming, and includes the Craig Thomas Discovery and Visitor Center. This will put you at the southern end of the Teton Park Road you bypassed earlier, and it provides a wonderful opportunity to make a loop and see even more of the park.

The Teton Park Road is 20 miles long and will take you past Jenny Lake and the visitor center there as well as several hiking options. But this is not a highway, and travel will be a bit slower before the road returns you to the Jackson Lake Junction. There are multiple scenic turnouts along this route as well, so if you have the time it's worth doing.

YELLOWSTONE ADVENTURES BY REGION

We always believe that the best way to enjoy the parks is to get out of your car and on the trails, but everyone has a different comfort level when it comes to outdoor recreation. This portion of the book covers, by region, activities that we have done ourselves, and provides insights that should help you choose which adventures are best for your family.

GEYSER REGION

The name says it all: this is where you will find the greatest concentration of geothermal features, including the famous Old Faithful. You will want to leave time for visiting at least some of the developed geothermal areas like Midway Geyser

The trail to Mystic Falls

Basin, with Grand Prismatic Spring (the biggest and most colorful); Biscuit Basin; and, of course, Old Faithful. However, sometimes the best way to see these features is to go beyond the boardwalks and hike to better vantages or even hidden features away from the crowds. A couple great hikes to waterfalls in this area also provide good views of the geyser basins, and this kind of hike often takes you to geysers that have never had roads built right up to their edges. The terrain in and around these basins tends to be mostly level, so even hikes of longer mileage are doable because you don't have to strain up and down hills. All of which makes this is a great region to exercise your legs and see the types of sights that only Yellowstone can provide.

Hiking

 **Mystic Falls**

This pleasant, short hike takes you to a beautiful waterfall and offers excellent views of the Firehole River and Upper Geyser

Strikingly beautiful Sapphire Pool

Mystic Falls from a distance

Basin area. Start by exploring the Biscuit Basin hydrothermal area, and from the end of the boardwalks continue just 1 more mile along a beautiful stream to arrive at the falls. Biscuit Basin includes the gorgeous Sapphire Pool, as well as several geysers that erupt constantly, even if they're somewhat small.

Distance: 2.5 miles roundtrip, with little elevation gain if you take the lower path or moderate gain if you take the upper trail for views of the Upper Geyser Basin

Time: 1 hour; add about 30 minutes more for the upper loop

Starting point: The trailhead is at the back side of the Biscuit Basin geyser area, which is just a couple miles north of the Old Faithful complex and well marked by road signs. Biscuit Basin has a network of boardwalks to view the geothermal features; but if you want to hike to the falls, you will leave the boardwalks and start down the trail that begins at the point of the boardwalks farthest from the parking area.

GPS (for parking lot): Latitude 44°29'6.26"N and Longitude 110°51'8.27"W

The trailhead is easy to find. Simply park in the paved lot, cross the Firehole River on the wooden bridge, and then take your time exploring Biscuit Basin, which includes Sapphire Pool and numerous other features. At the back of the geyser area, the boardwalk continues into the trees, where it turns to a dirt path, and soon you arrive at the trailhead marker. After you leave here to walk to the falls, you will soon be faced with a choice: you can take either the direct path upstream to the falls or the upper loop, which climbs to a small bluff where you are treated to great views of the Upper Geyser Basin and Firehole River.

There are many beautiful spots along the river, with small meadows and side canyons and a good number of wildflowers early in the summer. And you don't have far to go before you can see the impressive Mystic Falls.

Lone Star Geyser

This easy trail along a gorgeous, crystal-clear stream ends at the impressive Lone Star Geyser, which erupts roughly every three hours. The trail is an old service road and is actually paved; but at only one lane, it doesn't make you feel like you're walking down a street so much as taking an easy stroll through the woods. Even though the total distance is almost 5 miles, the trail's condition and the lack of elevation gain make this a trip almost anyone can do. There are also options for continuing on for a longer hike.

Distance: 4.8 miles roundtrip, negligible elevation gain
Time: 2.5–3.5 hours
Starting point: From the overpass exit to Old Faithful on the Grand Loop Road, travel east 2.5 miles to the turnoff very close to Kepler Cascades on the south side of the Grand Loop Road. The trailhead is at a small parking area with vault toilets.
GPS (for trailhead): Latitude 44°26'40.69"N and Longitude 110°48'16.35"W

Lone Star Geyser! (NPS photo)

The trail follows the Firehole River upstream through some of the prettiest forest, meadow, and streamside habitat that you could imagine. The river itself is stunningly clear, and if you're like Harley you'll wish you'd brought your fly rod. Since the trail is paved, you could do this hike in walking shoes just as well as hiking boots.

At the geyser itself is a logbook where people have recorded its eruptions. This information can help you make a pretty good estimate of when the next eruption will be, and you can plan accordingly. If it's soon, get out your snacks or lunch and wait until it erupts. If it's longer, continue down the trail to find beautiful meadows, a log bridge across the river, and some small geothermal features that all lie within a fifteen-minute walk. Just make sure you get back in time for the next eruption, because the Lone Star Geyser is impressive. The cone itself is about 6 feet high, and it sends water and steam 25–45 feet higher when it erupts, often displaying a nice rainbow when the sun is out. Don't forget to let your kids record the eruption

Don't forget to stop and rest once in a while, even on the easy trail to Lone Star Geyser.

in the logbook; they will think it's fun to be a part of leaving that data behind for the next group of hikers.

 ### Fairy Falls and Imperial Geyser

This hike has it all: the most colorful hot spring in the park (Grand Prismatic), a beautiful waterfall, and an active geyser off the beaten path in a scenic location. The trail is well worn and easy to follow, with almost no elevation gain, so the walking is easy even if the miles add up.

Distance: 5 miles roundtrip to Fairy Falls, 6.5 roundtrip to include Imperial Geyser
Time: 3–4 hours
Starting point: The Fairy Falls trailhead is at the turnoff on the west side of the road about 1.5 miles south of the large Midway Geyser

Basin parking area. If you're headed north, it is 2 miles north of the Biscuit Basin parking area.

GPS (trailhead parking): Latitude 44°30'54.86"N and Longitude 110°49'56.98"W

The trail leaves the Fairy Falls parking lot and immediately crosses the Firehole River on a steel trestle bridge as it heads north. This portion of the trail is an old gravel service road (Fountain Freight Road), so it's flat and broad and in good condition. As you walk along the Firehole River you have views of the Midway Geyser Basin, and after about two-thirds of a mile the hills on your left come right to the edge of the trail. Photographers long used the hill above the trail to take pictures of Grand Prismatic Spring, and it used to have many "social trails" leading across its face, but in recent years the National Park Service has closed it for rehabilitation. They plan to make an official trail to this very popular spot so that people can continue to take photos of this amazing natural pool!

Imperial Geyser

Fairy Falls possesses a more subtle beauty.

Take some photos and then continue on. Just a third of a mile farther you will come to an intersection with the Fairy Falls trail, which is where you leave Fountain Freight Road and turn left (west) to head toward the falls. This area was part of the big fire in 1988, so you soon enter a forest of fairly thick second-growth trees. The trail pleasantly meanders, along the base of the hills to your left and the level terrain of Fountain Flats to your right. After 1.5 miles you reach Fairy Falls, which is relatively small in volume but about 200 feet in height, making for a beautiful and delicate waterfall.

The area immediately below and surrounding the base of the falls is littered with fallen logs of every shape and size, which provide myriad options for sitting down and enjoying a picnic lunch or snack. Here you have the option of turning around and heading back or continuing 0.75 mile farther to check out some really neat thermal features.

As you continue, the forest becomes more open, with some meadows and aspen trees mixed in. If the weather is cool you will see steam ahead of you that marks your destination, and shortly you will arrive at Spray Geyser. This name is a little misleading, as the geyser is really more of a hot spring, but the colors of the algae mats are good. The trail continues on to the real reward, which is Imperial Geyser. It actually follows the runoff from this geyser, so you're hiking along a small stream of warm water where everything is colored from the thermophilic algae. This builds anticipation until you arrive at a beautiful hot spring with a lovely blue pool and an active geyser spouting off in the far corner. The kids really enjoyed seeing these features close up in such a pristine location. It's well worth the extra effort to make it here!

Bicycling

This region offers some of the best options for getting on a bike, especially because the only place to rent a bike is close by at Old Faithful Snow Lodge. The first option is to ride your bike 2.5 miles in each direction to Lone Star Geyser. This is a beautiful paved trail we have hiked, so you can see our trip report earlier in this section for more details. The second option is to ride 4 miles in each direction on Fountain Freight Road. This dirt and gravel road leaves the Fairy Falls trailhead parking area and goes north past Grand Prismatic Spring to the Lower Geyser Basin, where you ride along the shores of Goose Lake and are sure to see plenty of bison beside steaming thermal features. It ends at Fountain Flat Drive, where you could shuttle with a vehicle or simply turn around and head back on this flat and scenic old road.

MAMMOTH REGION

This is the only part of the park that stays open year-round, and it's where the initial developments in the park were built, so the Mammoth Hot Springs complex is quite developed. They chose this spot for a good reason: the hot springs' massive travertine terraces are unlike anything else you have ever seen. You will definitely want to spend time on the boardwalks and scenic drives through different portions of the hot springs, but if you have time for a little adventure, we have some good suggestions below—including one that requires you to bring your bathing suit! There are also quite a few hikes in this area that we did not recommend because they have too much distance and elevation gain for most kids, but they would be great trips to add a little challenge for teenagers or families with a lot of hiking experience (we recommend Lava Creek, Blacktail Deer Creek, or even Sepulcher Mountain for the really adventurous). You can find more information on these hikes at the visitor center.

Hiking

 Boiling River

A chance to soak in a natural hot spring in a beautiful location? Don't miss this!

Distance: An easy 1 mile roundtrip with no elevation gain
Time: A 10-minute walk, then soak as long as you care to!
Starting point: From the Mammoth Hot Springs intersection, it's almost exactly 2 miles north on the North Entrance Road to the Boiling River parking lot. The parking lot is practically on the Montana–Wyoming border and is on both sides of the road, so you can't miss it.
GPS: Latitude 44°59'33.02"N and Longitude 44°59'33.02"N

Come on in; the water's fine at Boiling River!

We often say that kids like to experience the outdoors in a more "hands on" way. Well, this is a chance to not only get your hands on nature but to soak your whole body in it. It is illegal (and dangerous!) to swim in any of Yellowstone's hydrothermal features. But here you're actually swimming in the Gardner River where the runoff from a hot spring enters it. This is completely within the rules, and absolutely delightful. If you have never soaked in a natural hot spring, this is your chance.

The trail starts up the river from the parking area, right next to the vault toilets, and it's basically a sidewalk in terms of width. After a short half-mile walk, you will see people soaking in the river, but if you walk past them the trail doubles back and arrives at a spot with room to take off your shoes and hang a towel and any extra layers you were wearing.

Soaking in hot springs is a great way to unwind.

Because the hot water from the side stream is mixing with the river water, temperatures fluctuate to some degree. But they always range from comfortable to delightful, and you can get warmer or cooler by changing your position relative to the incoming stream.

When we arrived at the parking area, there were so many cars that people were parking on the sides of the main road. But we need not have worried, because the swimming area is large enough to accommodate a lot of people.

This is a great way to relax after a long day of hiking, and our boys could not get enough. This really was one of the highlights of the whole trip for them. In fact, we planned to only go once, but they begged for more! Find a way to fit this in your schedule, and you won't be disappointed.

 ## Wraith Falls

An easy hike anyone can do, Wraith Falls is perfect for younger kids or if you're looking for something a little less strenuous.

Distance: An easy 1 mile roundtrip with minimal elevation gain
Time: 30 minutes
Starting point: The Wraith Falls trailhead is a short distance east of Mammoth Hot Springs, on the south side of Grand Loop Road between the Lava Creek picnic site/trailhead and the Blacktail Deer Creek trailhead.
GPS: Latitude 44°56'31.70"N and Longitude 110°37'25.13"W

If you're tired of being in the car and are looking for a quick hike to a pretty place, then make a stop at Wraith Falls. The trailhead is on a pullout on the main loop road, so getting in and out is fast.

The waterfall may not be the most spectacular in terms of volume or height, but instead of falling straight down a large drop, it actually slides over a smooth, exposed piece of rock, creating an interesting visual effect.

Wraith Falls can feel a little spooky.

The trail starts out flat through a meadow; it can be wet at times, so much of the trail is on boardwalk. Kids often find it delightful to run along the boardwalk or "tightrope walk" on the wooden edges. You walk through a thick forest for a short distance, and as you start to notice a large meadow ahead and to the right, you cross a wooden bridge over a small creek. You're almost there, because this is the stream that makes Wraith Falls. The trail moves ahead a short distance and then hooks left and starts climbing up a side canyon that includes stairs in places. At the top of these stairs you get your view of the falls.

 **Beaver Ponds Loop**

Distance: 5-mile loop
Time: 2.5–3.5 hours
Starting point: This loop has two trailheads, but both are right in the Mammoth Hot Springs complex. To travel clockwise, look for the boardwalks on the limestone terraces near the Liberty Cap formation. You will find the trailhead on the side closer to the general store. For the other trailhead, park near the Yellowstone Justice Center and walk behind the buildings to where you see an old road with a trail next to it. Be sure to take the trail, because the road will lead you somewhere else.

This is a popular hike that has a little bit of everything: forest, sage, views, ponds, and—at the right times of day—wildlife. It has a little elevation gain, but not much, and is easily accessible right out of Mammoth Hot Springs. The ponds are beautiful, and the views extend out across the Gardner River valley to the steep, dry sides of Mount Everts on the opposite side.

 **Bunsen Peak**

Distance: This is an out-and-back to the top of a peak, 4.2 miles roundtrip with a substantial 1300-foot elevation gain. This hike is considered moderately strenuous; you have to earn the views at the top!
Time: 2–3 hours
Starting point: The trailhead is on the east side of Grand Loop Road 5 miles south of Mammoth Hot Springs. The road climbs as it heads south from the springs and then goes through Kingman Pass before leveling out. This is where you will find the trailhead, which is also across the road from the Glen Creek trailhead. If you see Swan Lake on your right, you have gone a bit too far.

Horse trip from Glen Creek trailhead (NPS/Jim Peaco photo)

The challenging ascent leads to amazing views from the top. Bunsen is the highest peak in this area of the park, so you can see a long way in every direction. On the downside, kids are rarely as interested in views as adults are, and there is a lot of communications equipment on top of this peak supplying the Mammoth area with phone service and the like, degrading the wilderness aspect a bit. But still—majestic views!

Horseback Rides

At stables a short distance south from Mammoth Hot Springs, you can hire guided horseback rides of one or two hours. Get more information and make your reservations with Xanterra.

Bicycling

Just south of Mammoth Hot Springs, Bunsen Peak Road overlooks a portion of the Gardner River. This trail, 6 miles each way, is closed to vehicle traffic, making it a much safer option than biking on the road. The downside is that bicycle rentals are only offered through Xanterra at Old Faithful Snow Lodge, a great distance away. You will need to plan ahead if you want to do this option and don't have your own bikes.

Rafting

Whitewater rafting is not available in the park, but if you're looking to experience floating on a river, numerous guide services offer trips on the Yellowstone River right where it exits the park in Gardiner, Montana. A quick internet search on rafting in Gardiner will get you started.

TOWER REGION

The Tower Region is the crown jewel of Yellowstone for wildlife viewing. It is lower in elevation, with more sage and grassland for large ungulates to feed on, so you'll find bison, elk, antelope, and deer in abundance here. And because they are here, the wolves are here also. This is a go-to destination for trying to spot these elusive animals. But it isn't just the number of animals, it is also the terrain. The wide-open vistas make it easier to spot game at a distance, something harder to do in the forested regions farther south in the park. These same vistas also make for excellent hiking opportunities if you like amazing views with your walk. We have selected a few of our favorites to share with you. These are by no means the only hikes in this region, but we feel that they are the ones best suited to exploring with kids, whether you want something easy, moderate, or a bit challenging to help them grow their confidence.

Hiking

 Trout Lake

A short hike to a beautiful lake makes for a great picnic or just a quick getaway to enjoy the outdoors.

Distance: About 0.3 mile each way to the lake, or 1 mile total as a loop around the lake

Time: 15–20 minutes hiking each direction; as much time as you like at the lake

Starting point: The trailhead parking area is on the north side of the Northeast Entrance Road, about 1.2 miles west of the Pebble Creek Campground access road.

GPS: Latitude 44°53'56.95"N and Longitude 110° 7'22.61"W

The lake is nestled in a little bowl with pine trees on the near side and a sage-covered bench on the far side where you can spot wildlife in the mornings and evenings. The bench rises farther into pine-covered slopes ending in impressive cliffs that reflect perfectly in the clear surface of the lake. The water is so clear that you can sometimes spot the trout swimming below the surface.

Placid Trout Lake is a great spot for wildlife watching.

The hike itself is not long, but it's fairly steep in stretches. Fortunately there is good reason to take breaks along the way: the views looking back across the canyon are gorgeous.

A trail circles the lake, and some fishermen will likely be using it to try their luck. If you go clockwise upon reaching the lake, you soon come to a wooden bridge that crosses its outlet. After we ate our picnic lunch, our boys enjoyed playing on this bridge and watching the water cascade over the moss-covered logs littering the creek bed. They thought the scene was so pretty that they insisted I take pictures of it. I suspected the photos would not come out well, but I obliged, because it wasn't about getting a great photo so much as the fact that they had found something beautiful and wanted to share it with me. Isn't that why we get out there?

Even if you have to huff and puff a little up the hill, most anyone can do this hike. The beauty of the lake and the views all along the way make this short but sweet hike worth doing, especially if you bring a meal or a snack to enjoy while you soak in the scenery. And if it's later in the summer and you catch a grasshopper along the trail, you will have a meal to share with the hungry trout in the lake!

Finally, if you have the time and want a little adventure, head off trail in a northeasterly direction parallel to the road to find neighboring Buck Lake, less than a fifth of a mile from the eastern shore of Trout Lake.

 Petrified Forest of Specimen Ridge

This hike demands a lot of effort, but if you're up for it, you and your kids should find the payoffs worth it. This is one of the rare places in Yellowstone where your children can actually touch the feature they're looking at, which is just what kids love!

Distance: 3 miles roundtrip, with a lot of elevation gain
Time: 1.5–2 hours up, 1 hour down. Allow at least 30 minutes for exploring the petrified forest once you're there. The hike is considered very strenuous and is appropriate for fit children ages eight and up.
Starting point: The trailhead parking area is on the south side of Northeast Entrance Road, 4.5 miles east of Tower Junction. If you're headed east on Northeast Entrance Road and cross the bridge over the Lamar River, you have gone 0.25 mile too far.
GPS: Latitude 44°54'42.52"N and Longitude 110°19'40.55"W

From the parking lot, look south toward Specimen Ridge. The nearest open hilltop in front of you holds the first petrified tree, which is lying down, but the larger collection of massive standing trees is higher and farther to the right, past the group of live trees on the next open ridge. The yellow dotted line in the photo opposite gives a very rough idea of where the trail leads after beginning to the left of the photo and then entering the trees. Once in the trees, the trail goes left to the backside of the ridge and then switches back to emerge on the top of the ridge where the arrow depicts the location of the "first tree." From here the trail follows the ridge farther up before cutting through a copse of trees and emerging on the second open ridge, marked "Petrified Forest." This is your ultimate destination.

The trail starts out on an old two-track dirt road through the sage-covered flat, then veers right toward the ridge and into the trees. This is not a maintained or marked Park Service trail, but rather what is often called a "social trail." Still, it's sanctioned by the Park Service and popular enough that the trail is well defined and easy to follow.

You begin by crossing a large sage flat, but the trail starts to climb quite rapidly after half a mile, before entering the trees. Here you will want to follow the most obvious trail as it veers left, even though your ultimate destination lies to the right. Stay

First tree   Petrified Forest

The route to the Petrified Forest

Stopping to take in the view from Specimen Ridge

on the trail to maintain a manageable rate of climb. It snakes through the trees and then breaks out into a second open area of sage before veering right and back toward the main ridge. As you crest the ridge, you will be greeted with commanding views of the Lamar River valley and the distant Buffalo Plateau.

Better still, just on the other side of this spot you will find your first petrified tree. This one is lying on its side and may look like a rock at first, but your kids will soon recognize it for what it is and be fascinated with the opportunity to see and touch it. Take a little time for a rest break and to enjoy the sense of discovery. Another stump is visible slightly farther down the slope, and if you're tuckered out you could simply turn around here to make this a shorter trip.

But if this first discovery has whetted your appetite for more, the real payoff lies about 20 minutes up the trail.

Look left and follow the trail uphill along the ridge. As you look up, you will see a grassy open ridge and trees growing in the small basin to the right. The good news is that you don't have to climb the entire ridge. The trail will climb for a good 10 minutes or so, but it will veer right and into the trees before reaching the top. The trail angles uphill through the trees before emerging at the crest of the adjacent ridge, and here you will find the petrified trees. It's a collection of stumps and tree trunks, some of which are six feet in diameter and others that are narrower but eight to ten feet tall, scattered down along the open face of this ridge. Take time to explore them, but be careful, as the slope is very steep and composed of loose rocks that make slipping and sliding easy to do. Wear good shoes or boots. On the downhill side the petrified roots of one tree were exposed, which was really high on the kids' coolness scale.

Our boys loved seeing these petrified trees, and it took me a little bit by surprise how fascinated they were after the challenging hike. While I had seen petrified wood before, this was all new to them, and they reacted as though they had made some great discovery—which of course they had.

Young explorers by a massive petrified stump

Garnet Hill Loop

This is a fairly long hike, but the terrain is mostly gentle, so you shouldn't find it too challenging. It offers good wildlife-viewing opportunities and shows you beautiful and seldom-seen parts of the Yellowstone River with stunning views of the wilderness areas to the north of the park.

Distance: 7.5 miles roundtrip with little elevation gain, making this a moderate hike
Time: 4–5 hours
Starting point: This trailhead is very easy to find because it is right at Tower Junction. Park in the large lot just east of the service station at this intersection and walk a short distance (400 yards) on Northeast Entrance Road to the trailhead on your left.

Since this is a loop you can do it in either direction. Typically the day will get warmer during your hike, so take the loop counterclockwise to spend the warmest part of the day in the shady confines of Elk Creek. This is how we did it, and it's the direction of the description that follows.

From the parking lot, walk about 400 yards down Northeast Entrance Road until the road starts to drop down into a shallow canyon. On the left here you should see a large wooden sign marking the trailhead. The trail leaves the road and follows the edge of a large meadow for about half a mile then cuts right and gains slight elevation while climbing the modest sage-covered

The panoramic views from the Garnet Hill Loop trail are awe-inspiring

Overlooking the Yellowstone River

ridge that has been on your right all this time. On the other side of this ridge lies the Yellowstone River. Once you reach the top, you can look upstream to its confluence with the Lamar River, although the layout of the river canyons does not make this obvious.

For the next 4 miles the trail basically parallels and follows the river downstream, gradually getting closer to the water and lower in elevation until the trail lies right on the banks of the river. As you drop, you go from the exposed ridge down through some shallow side canyons and begin to encounter more trees. Right before joining the river, you drop quickly through a pine forest and emerge in a beautiful meadow that often has wildlife at the right times of day. If you haven't stopped already, the shady bank overlooking the river and the Buffalo Plateau beyond is a good place to take a break and have a snack.

The kids enjoy the Garnet Hill Loop Trail.

From here the trail follows the river for a half mile or so before starting the only section with significant elevation gain. There are a few switchbacks here, but the climb is pretty short-lived, and with each turn you get better and better views of the surrounding terrain.

As the river bends to the west, rock outcroppings are fun for kids to climb on and make for great photo ops.

At this point the trail heads downhill until it reaches Elk Creek and an intersection with the Hellroaring Trail. In one direction, this trail crosses the creek and switchbacks up a steep and open grade to the loop road where the trailhead is located. In the other, it continues downhill to a bridge that crosses the Yellowstone River, then on to the creek that shares its name. But you don't want to do either of those. Instead, once you arrive at Elk Creek, stay on the near (east) side of the creek and start following it upstream. Soon you will come to a small and scenic waterfall and a little bit steeper climb, but after that the trail levels out.

As the trail continues upstream, it's mostly in the shady creek bottom, alternating between thicker bands of forest and small, open meadows lush with green growth that attracts the elk the creek is named after. One log bridge crosses the creek. Although you are gaining elevation, it's mostly so gradual that you won't give it much notice.

After about 2 miles of moving up the creek bottom, you come upon a large meadow. Soon you see a manmade structure at the edge of it. This is the cookout shelter where stagecoach trips from Roosevelt Lodge head for their outdoor steak dinners. The trail stays in the middle of the meadow and passes within a couple hundred yards of the shelter, eventually merging into the dirt road that services the cook shelter. The easiest option here is to follow the road all the way back to Tower Junction and your vehicle, but an alternate trail crosses the meadow just before its narrowest part and rejoins the trail that you began on.

One last thought: the meadow looks level and inviting, so you might be tempted to cross it off-trail to get back to the starting point, but don't! Not only is it not as easy as it looks—it's also against park rules, and for good reason! The meadows won't benefit from having hikers tromp across them—and wild animals may be foraging, hidden by the small rises. Stay on the trails; you'll be happier that way!

 **Lost Lake**

Distance: 4-mile loop
Time: 2–3 hours
Starting point: Find the trailhead behind Roosevelt Lodge.

If you are looking for something less challenging than the hikes we described above, this easier trail still passes by a beautiful lake and has some nice views from the ridgetop. Be aware there is a lot of horse traffic and you can also drive to its midpoint in your car. But if you're OK with that, it is still a beautiful area—it just doesn't merit a full description.

The trail climbs a ridge, where it joins a horse trail before reaching the good-sized lake after just a half mile or so. If you have younger kids, you could simply go to the lake and enjoy some time there and then turn around. If you're looking for a little more, continue past the lake and arrive at the Petrified Trees parking lot. After passing the tree, the trail continues on the other side of the parking lot and goes east back toward the lodge, passing close to the Tower Ranger Station.

 **Slough Creek**

Distance: 4 miles roundtrip, or more if you choose
Time: 1–3 hours each way
Starting point: The trail starts on the road heading into Slough Creek Campground, adjacent to the first vault toilet you come to as you near the camping area.

This popular hiking trail is also less challenging than some of the others we've described. It's popular with fishermen and wildlife watchers and takes you to a beautiful meadow with Slough Creek flowing through it. It gets a bit more traffic because of this and because it gets a lot of horse traffic from Silver Ranch, which lies just outside the park boundary and has a permit to bring horses into the park for guest rides. But these aren't major concerns, so if you're looking for somsething shorter and relatively easy, this could be a great option.

The trail has some moderate climbing for the first mile as you crest the ridge, then levels out and drops into the Slough Creek river bottom. After 2 miles you approach the creek in a large meadow that is noted for wildlife sightings and great trout fishing. This could be your turnaround point, but if you're feeling ambitious, another 2.5 miles takes you to a second and even larger meadow. This one you can follow all the way to the northern border of the park.

Horseback and Wagon Rides

If you're hoping for equine activities with an Old West theme, then this region of the park offers your best bet. The Roosevelt Lodge area is near one of Theodore Roosevelt's old hunting

Stagecoach ride from Roosevelt

camps, and it has a distinctly western feel to it. At the stables here you can find guided horseback rides of one or two hours in length. In addition, there are options for stagecoach rides by themselves and wagon rides out to a dinner site where they will feed you delicious steaks in an outdoor shelter. Both of these activities are offered by Xanterra Parks & Resorts, and their website has more information and instructions for making reservations. These options aren't inexpensive, but the stagecoach ride by itself is surprisingly affordable. Your kids will love it.

CANYON REGION

This region is named after one of the most spectacular features of the park, the Grand Canyon of the Yellowstone. In any trip to the park, make sure to devote at least a few hours to viewing this canyon, as it is breathtaking enough to be the very reason they

The Grand Canyon of the Yellowstone is pretty amazing in its own right.

called this place *Yellow*stone. You don't need to be a hiker to see it; there are roads on both rims of the canyon and many pullouts with accessible paths to most of the best views. But if you do want to stretch your legs, we have suggestions that will take you to some unique vistas. One we left out is the Howard Eaton Trail, which takes you to a series of lakes: Cascade, Grebe, Wolf, and Ice, with a side trip to Observation Peak. We didn't include it because this trail is so heavily forested it can leave kids with the sense that the scenery never changes, and it is often wet and muddy through July, which means a lot of biting insects. But all the lakes are pretty, and these trails are popular; if you're interested, you can find more information at the visitor center.

Hiking

Lily Pad and Ribbon Lakes

This is a great place for a picnic when you're checking out the south rim of the Grand Canyon of the Yellowstone. It's also a nice short hike, with spectacular views of the canyon, that ends at a beautiful spot. The trail lies right on the canyon's edge, and there are no guardrails, so parents of young kids will want to lay some ground rules to protect them. It's also a good idea to carry bug spray, since you will be near a lake.

Distance: 1.6 miles roundtrip with negligible elevation gain to Lily Pad Lake; 3.8 miles roundtrip if you continue to Ribbon Lake and back
Time: 1.5–2 hours to Lily Pad; 2.5–3.5 hours for Ribbon
Starting point: Turn off Grand Loop Road onto South Rim Drive just a couple miles south of Canyon Junction. Take South Rim Drive all the way to its terminus at Artist Point. Walk to the circular path at the point and find the trailhead at the back of the circle.
GPS (trailhead): Latitude 44°43'16.01"N and Longitude 110°28'43.84"W

If you're looking for a small adventure after viewing Lower Falls from Artist Point on the south rim of the Grand Canyon of

The serenity of Lily Pad Lake meadow

the Yellowstone, take the trail that leads downstream from the point. Your trip can easily be extended to longer distances and other lakes if you're feeling up to it.

The path weaves in and out of the trees, but most of the time it's right along the rim of the canyon, affording amazing views of the brilliantly colored cliffs. If you're nervous about having your kids near big drop-offs, you may not enjoy this portion of the trail. Remind your kids beforehand that they need to stay close to you or a certain distance from the edge. The trail continues like this for a little over half a mile and then turns right, away from the canyon edge, and climbs a small ridge. From the turn it is a mere 0.2 mile to the near edge of Lily Pad Lake, although you will want to continue another 0.1 mile for the best locations on the lakeshore.

Find a spot along the lake, have a snack, and let the kids look for bugs and frogs and throw twigs or rocks in the water. When you are ready, you can head back the way you came or continue on to a larger lake, Ribbon Lake, in a more open area. This lake is another 1.1 miles farther along on a trail that stays

The Lower Falls on Uncle Tom's Trail are spectacular—and chilly.

in the trees until you reach your destination, at which point portions of the lake are bordered by large meadows. You can also take a short side hike from Ribbon Lake to the side of the canyon for more breathtaking views.

Uncle Tom's Trail

A set of metal stairs bolted into the side of the canyon lets visitors see spectacular Lower Falls up close and personal. Your legs will burn as you climb back up, but the views are worth it.

Distance: Steep and short at less than 1 mile; 328 stairs help the trail descend 500 feet toward the base of the Lower Falls

Time: 1 hour

Starting point: A couple miles south of Canyon Junction, leave Grand Loop Road and turn onto South Rim Drive. Cross the Yellowstone River and pass a parking area on your right. Continue another quarter mile or so and take the first left to the parking area there. Walk downstream on the South Rim Trail until you see signs for Uncle Tom's Trail.

GPS (trailhead): Latitude 44°42'58.93"N and Longitude 10°29'42.20"W

The Lower Falls of the Grand Canyon of the Yellowstone

After you encounter a sign marking the start of Uncle Tom's Trail, you descend on a few switchbacks, and then the stairs begin—all 328 of them. Keep dropping down these metal stairs with glimpses of the canyon as you go. Once you reach the bottom, you receive the payoff: a great view of Lower Falls. You are so close to the falls that you're often sprayed and misted. It can be a bit chilly, so you may want to bring sweatshirts or light jackets for the kids. Once you're done taking pictures, head back. This is where the work really begins!

 North Rim Trail

This trail offers some of the best views of the Grand Canyon of the Yellowstone, which we consider a must-see for any visit here. You can just as easily drive to each of these viewpoints; the trail is usually within 50 yards of the road, except for one section where there are no views.

Distance: 2.5 miles from the brink of Lower Falls to Inspiration Point, with a small elevation gain unless you drop down to the several viewpoints

Time: 1.5–2.5 hours

Starting point: The North Rim Trail can be accessed from a number of spots along North Rim Drive, the turnoff for which is about a mile south of Canyon Junction on the Grand Loop Road.

Accessible from a number of different spots on North Rim Drive, this trail is a pleasant walk between numerous viewpoints with little real elevation change. If parking is limited, hiking may be the best way to see all the viewpoints without having to fight for a spot. Otherwise, the best option is to drive between them and spend your energy walking to some of the viewpoints lower down in the canyon. The section leading out to Inspiration Point does get away from the road and makes for a peaceful and beautiful walk, but unfortunately it eventually comes out at a busy parking lot.

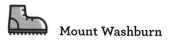 **Mount Washburn**

Distance: 5 or 6.2 miles roundtrip, depending on which trailhead you use, with a strenuous 1400 feet of elevation gain
Time: 3–6 hours
Starting point: Take Grand Loop Road north from Canyon Junction to the trailhead at Dunraven Pass. From here, this trail is 3.1 miles each way to the top. Or drive another 5.8 miles (10.3 miles total from Canyon Junction) and turn right on Chittenden Road to the parking lot at the end. From here, it is 2.5 miles each way.

If you have older kids and are fit, this might be an option for you. No matter which starting point you choose, the trail climbs through alpine terrain dotted with wildflowers and bighorn sheep to a summit with expansive views and a fire lookout on top. This hike is big on effort, scenery, and, as one of the park's most popular hikes, people. Be prepared to deal with crowds.

Horseback Riding

A stable at Canyon Village provides one- and two-hour horseback rides through the woods and meadows surrounding the village. These trips do not include views of the Grand Canyon of the Yellowstone but are still scenic. This stable is operated by Xanterra, and more information can be found on their website.

LAKE REGION

Yellowstone Lake is huge, and your travels through the park will most likely take you on a drive along its shores for some expansive panoramas. The sea kayaking, guided cruises, and fishing boats at the lake are great ways to get out on the water. There are also beautiful hikes along its shores, where just a few miles will get you enough elevation gain to witness some broad views of the lake and surrounding region from above. We will also include a caution here: if you're considering the Riddle Lake Trail, keep in mind that it is closed until July 15 each year because it is in a grizzly management zone. Even later in the summer, it's recommended that you hike in groups of four or more for safety, so we left it off our list. But there are many other good options so get out there and enjoy.

Hiking

Pelican Creek Nature Trail

A short and scenic trail with a wide variety of habitats and nice views of Yellowstone Lake and the Pelican Creek estuary, this is a great place for birding. It's also an excellent choice for a picnic.

Pause to look around as you walk the Pelican Creek Nature Trail.

Look for birds at the Pelican Creek estuary.

Distance: An easy 1.3-mile loop with no elevation gain, very close to Fishing Bridge

Time: 30 minutes to 1 hour

Starting point: The trail leaves from the south side of East Entrance Road at the west end of the Pelican Creek bridge, 1 mile east of the Fishing Bridge Visitor Center.

GPS (trailhead parking lot): Latitude 44°33'36.13"N and Longitude 110°21'38.55"W

If you are anywhere near the north end of the lake and looking for a quick chance to stretch your legs or have a picnic, this is an excellent choice. The trail leaves the parking area on East Entrance Road and heads into trees that border the Pelican Creek estuary. Soon it splits into a loop and you have two choices: go left to stay near the estuary, or go right and deeper into the forest. Since it's a loop you will eventually see both, so there are no wrong choices!

The trail eventually reaches the shores of Yellowstone Lake, where kids can throw and skip stones into the water, scramble on huge driftwood logs, or even splash a bit on warmer days.

The forest abuts the shore a mere 20 yards away from the lake's edge and provides shady spots to set up a picnic and gaze at the lake while watching your kids play on the beach. The only thing to look out for is windy days when the breeze coming off the lake might make a picnic at water's edge a bit less enjoyable.

 Natural Bridge Trail

If you're looking for a short and easy hike to a pretty area with an attractive natural bridge made of rhyolite rock, this could be the hike for you. Just be aware that the trail is on a paved service road that is also open to bikes. While the bridge lacks a lot of "wow" factor, this hike is a good option if you're looking for something less strenuous or are in need of leg-stretcher.

The views improve after you've been on the Natural Bridge Trail for a while.

The namesake Natural Bridge

Distance: 3 miles roundtrip, no elevation gain
Time: 1–2 hours
Starting point: The trailhead leaves from the Bridge Bay Marina parking lot. Drive close to the marina, but not all the way to the boat ramp, and park on the opposite side of the lot from the water's edge. A wooden sign marks the start of the trail, and it's easy to see. You will only walk a couple hundred yards before you approach a campground where a second wooden sign points left to where you continue down the trail.
GPS (traihead): Latitude 44°32'1.77"N and Longitude 110°26'18.61"W

From the Bridge Bay Marina parking lot, the trail heads toward the campground before swinging left around the marina and parking lot. For the first ten minutes of the hike, you are looking at the parking area on your left. It then enters a nice forest with good views of the bay before leaving the water and joining up with the service road. After this point you walk on a paved, single-lane road up the Bridge Creek drainage, which is quite pretty. After 0.7 mile you come to a canyon on your right where the natural bridge is high above you. There is an interpretive sign here, and the trail continues up steep switchbacks to the top of the cliff for closer views of the bridge, although walking on the bridge is not allowed. Our boys felt the bridge was interesting, but not enough to warrant the further climbing required to get closer.

 Elephant Back Trail

A medium-distance hike with a moderate elevation gain of 850 feet, Elephant Back Trail is not too easy and not too hard, with sweeping panoramic views of Yellowstone Lake and the Absaroka Range in the distance. It will be a little challenging for younger kids but still something they can tackle for that feeling of accomplishment when they reach the top. Without many other diversions to hold your attention as you go, you're basically enjoying a walk through the woods until you suddenly come to the viewpoint.

Distance: 3.6 miles roundtrip with a partial loop
Time: 2–3 hours
Starting point: The trailhead is on the west side of Grand Loop Road just 1 mile south of the Fishing Bridge Junction. If you reach the Lake Village turnoff, you've gone too far.
GPS: Latitude 44°33'24.33"N and Longitude 110°24'6.50"W

The trail leaves the road and briefly enters a wooded area before crossing a powerline right-of-way. You cross this quickly and then reenter the mature stand of timber. It was spared in the big fires of 1988, so the trees are older and widely spaced, giving the forest a welcoming and open feel.

Holy moly! Look at that view from Elephant Back!

After 1 mile the trail forks into a loop, with either way eventually leading to the top. The left fork is slightly shorter and therefore slightly steeper, so we went right. Going right also makes the approach to the viewpoint more sudden and thus more dramatic when you break out of the trees and see it for the first time. But you really can't go wrong either way.

It's also about the time the trail forks that it really starts to climb. It isn't excessive, but you will be puffing a bit; just stop for a quick breather as needed. You'll want to save snack time or your picnic for when you reach the top so you have more time to enjoy the view. Two benches up there give you a spot to rest while taking it all in.

A nice walk in the woods along a clear trail

 ## Storm Point Trail

Distance: 2.3-mile loop with no elevation gain. This area is often closed in late spring and early summer due to bear activity, so ask at the Fishing Bridge Visitor Center about the current conditions.
Time: 1–2 hours
Starting point: The trailhead is at the Indian Pond pullout on the south side of East Entrance Road, 3 miles east of the Fishing Bridge Visitor Center.
GPS: Latitude 44°33'34.76"N and Longitude 110°19'34.91"W

This trail is short and flat with a variety of terrain: woods, pond, and lakeshore. It begins by Indian Pond but soon veers right and into the forest. Eventually you emerge from the trees onto the windswept shore at Storm Point, with sweeping views of Yellowstone Lake and the Absaroka Range beyond. A nice bonus for kids (and adults, for that matter) is the colony of yellow-bellied marmots on the rocks near the point. These little critters always delight, but remember not to feed them, as they can become aggressive. One last consideration is the weather. As the name implies, this area can be quite windy, so make sure you're prepared.

Lake Overlook Trail

Distance: 2 miles roundtrip with 400 feet of elevation gain near the top
Time: 1–1.5 hours
Starting point: The Lake Overlook Trail leaves from the West Thumb Geyser Basin parking lot. As you enter the parking lot, the trailhead is immediately on your right, on the side of the parking lot farthest from the information station and the lake.

For a relatively short hike, Lake Overlook Trail packs in a lot of features. The hike begins in the lakeside forest of the West Thumb bay, crosses the main road, and then climbs a bit to a mountain meadow with views of Yellowstone Lake and points beyond. Along the way, backcountry thermal features provide a little sense of discovery, so the bang for your buck is pretty good here.

Duck Lake

Distance: 1 mile roundtrip with a minimal climb
Time: Less than 1 hour
Starting point: The trailhead is at the northern end of the West Thumb Geyser Basin parking lot.

If you're in the West Thumb area and looking for a picnic spot to eat lunch away from the crowds or a quick and easy chance to stretch your legs, consider Duck Lake. The trail crosses the road, climbs a small hill, then drops into a little bowl that holds Duck Lake, a short distance from the shores of Yellowstone Lake. The lake offers a beach where kids can play and skip stones, and there are enough trees to provide shady spots for lunch. On the way back you will see some powerlines, and if you follow those a short distance, you will get views of the West Thumb bay.

Boating

As you might guess from the name, the Lake Region offers real boating options—it's pretty much the only part of the park to do so. You can take scenic cruises on the lake or guided fishing trips for cutthroat and lake trout, or rent a boat or canoe to explore the shores of Yellowstone and Lewis lakes. A more adventurous option is to canoe up Lewis Lake to the Lewis River, then follow this stream upriver to larger Shoshone Lake, which is off-limits to motorized craft. This is the only stream in the park that you're allowed to float. We provide a few more details in the Fishing and Boating section in the Best Bets chapter.

Xanterra Parks & Resorts rents rowboats and outboards at Bridge Bay Marina. If you're looking for guided fishing trips or canoe or kayak rentals, quite a few outfitters provide them. Since they are constantly changing, the best way to locate them for your trip is simply to look online.

Ready to backpack!

YOUR FIRST YELLOWSTONE BACKPACKING TRIP

Backpacking in Yellowstone can seem daunting, what with the vast wilderness, the presence of bears, and the fairly involved permit process. But if you follow certain precautions, choose your routes wisely, and plan your trip far enough in advance, all of those concerns can be easily addressed, and you can enjoy a true wilderness adventure that gets to the heart of some of the best things the park has to offer. This chapter tells you what you need to know and suggests a number of good trip options suitable for kids.

There are 294 backcountry campsites in Yellowstone—sites you have to walk to, not drive to, and that you need a permit to

Beautiful sunsets are one of the reasons to backpack.

A view of Sentinel Meadows keeps you motivated to keep moving.

stay in. Many of the sites can be reserved months in advance by mailing an application to the backcountry office, while others can only be reserved in person within forty-eight hours of your trip. All the trips we recommend have campsites that can be reserved in advance, and to do so you should mail your application so that it arrives before March 31 since the random drawing and lottery to assign sites happens on April 1. Permits for applications received after that point will be issued on a first come, first served basis. More info can be found on the Yellowstone National Park backcountry website. Here, we describe the trips so you can decide if this is something you want to do with your family.

BACKPACKING AND BACKCOUNTRY CAMPING IN YELLOWSTONE

While the thought of strapping everything on your back that you and your kids might need for a couple of nights of sleeping outside may seem overwhelming, the challenge is so worth it. If you honestly evaluate your skills and the abilities of your weakest (or most vulnerable) member and decide everyone is up for

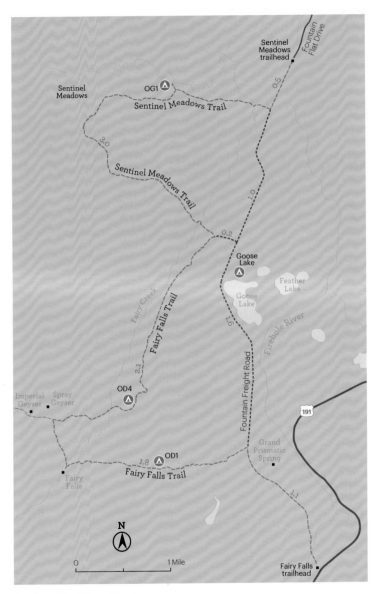

Sentinel Fairy Falls trail system

It's an easy trail near Goose Lake.

it, you will experience awesome rewards. Although a Google search will turn up a big pile of results, we found two sites to be the most helpful. A note of caution: these sites are not aimed specifically at taking kids into the backcountry. We looked for trips we felt our kids (and the adults carrying the extra gear) were up for and then made sure to implement kid-friendly strategies to help keep the kids going.

You will need to use the resources the national park website provides to understand rules and regulations, locate site numbers, find seasonal area closures, and more. Although the document with all of the campsites listed seems dense and quite unreadable, power through it to find the site you want. We give you site numbers for the sites we've visited and reviewed, but even the areas we've reviewed have other sites you may want to check out. You will also find the permit application on the Yellowstone backcountry web page. It is important to note that, even in this high-speed era, you must mail, fax, or hand deliver your permit application, as no online system exists for this right now. Get those permit applications done well in advance of the March 31 cutoff! (You can mail your permit application anytime, but you will stand a much better chance of a successful drawing if you get it in earlier.)

We also use the Trail Guides Yellowstone website for much of our trip planning. Its interactive map under Planning, in the Yellowstone Campgrounds section, is really helpful and intuitive. It presents a parkwide map showing all the backcountry campsites divided into regions. If you click on a region, a box will pop up with a photo and brief description. Click on this to go to the Regional page, which will give you a more detailed map, the site numbers, restrictions, and more. Go to their Hiking page and find the area you will be in to learn more about what type of hiking you will encounter. These detailed lists will also give you any backcountry sites along the trail. Finally, this company maintains a bunch of articles to help you get ready for your backcountry trip. You can find them under the Planning menu.

The hike to Fairy Falls takes you through a sea of gold.

Sentinel Meadows and Fairy Falls Area

These trips take you on a tour of the west side of the Lower Geyser Basin, where you will see active thermal features, expansive meadows, bison, geese, waterfalls, and surrounding mountains. It's a great option for kids because the valley you hike in is as flat as a pancake, and the trails are arranged in a figure-8 pattern with a 0.2-mile connector in the center, so you can choose whichever trips you like and customize the distance you will walk.

Distance: 2–11 miles roundtrip

Time: 1–3 days

Starting point: The Fountain Freight Road trailhead (Sentinel Meadows trailhead) is in the parking area at the end of Fountain Flat Drive in the Geyser Region. This road goes west from the Grand Loop Road between Madison Junction and Old Faithful, about 2 miles north of the Fountain Paint Pot parking lot.

GPS (parking lot and trailhead): Latitude 44°34'2.13"N and Longitude 110°50'6.43"W

Easy Trip Options

Perhaps you don't have a lot of specialized gear, so you're going to have a heavy pack, but you still want to have the experience of sleeping in a tent in the backcountry. Or you have smaller children and will therefore have to carry more than your share. This system of trails gives you options.

Starting from the trailhead at the end of Fountain Flat Drive, it is a short half-hour walk to the OG1 campsite. This camp offers big views of Sentinel Meadows and the thermal features there: Mound Spring, Flat Cone Spring, and Queens Laundry. It is also a great place for wildlife viewing, bison in particular. You could spend the night here and then head back the way you came, or spend the second day completing the upper loop

The Firehole River lazes along near some campsites.

of approximately 3 more miles as you return on Fountain Freight Road.

Fountain Freight Road is an old dirt and gravel route open only to hikers and bicyclists. It serves as the return route for all the trail system's hiking options, and it also includes a campsite along the way on the north shores of Goose Lake. This campsite is reserved for people with special needs or on bicycles, but anyone can use it if it's still not reserved a day or two ahead. Bicycling here with your family instead of hiking could provide an enjoyable alternative, and bicycles can be rented from Xanterra at the Old Faithful Snow Lodge. But even on foot, it's only 1.5 miles from the trailhead to this beautiful spot.

Moderate Trip Options

If you're willing to stretch your legs a bit further, the trail system's lower loop has more spectacular sites to see. Imperial Geyser is a special place, as is Fairy Falls. Both can be reached via a longer day hike from the south that begins at the Fairy Falls trailhead and follows Fountain Freight Road past Grand Prismatic Spring. But by coming in from the north, you can turn it into a nice, moderate overnight as well. Simply start down

Campsite OA1 is a dream location to set up camp.

Fountain Freight Road from the Sentinel Meadows trailhead at the end of Fountain Flat Drive, then turn west at the marked junction with Fairy Falls Trail before you reach Goose Lake. From here it's less than 2 miles to campsite OD4 (shown on page 123); or approximately 3 miles total for the day. On day two you can check out Imperial Geyser and Fairy Falls before heading back to the trailhead via Fountain Freight Road for a bit longer day of about 4.5 miles.

If you're OK with slightly more miles on your first day, you can do the upper loop to Sentinel Meadows before making your way to OD4 for a total of about 4.5 miles. This additional distance will take you to beautiful views of the basin, a high mountain lake with waterfowl, and almost guaranteed bison sightings, along with additional modest geothermal features. This is the way we approached it, and while the boys were very glad to reach camp, the challenge also gave them a real sense of accomplishment.

We did the hike counterclockwise, and this is the direction we would recommend. But if OD4 is unavailable, you could substitute campsite OD1, and hike the loop clockwise by continuing down Fountain Freight Road past Goose Lake. This campsite is in a heavily wooded area so it doesn't offer much in the way of views, but it is very private. The second day you would continue to Fairy Falls and Imperial Geyser and then continue on the lower loop and back to your car at the trailhead via Fountain Freight Road.

🥾 Lone Star Geyser Overnight

The trip to Lone Star Geyser makes for a nice day hike or bike ride (the trail is open to bicycles), but it can easily be extended slightly to make an excellent choice for an overnight trip. Details and photos of the hike to the geyser are in the Adventures section for the Geyser Region, but there are also a number of backcountry campsites available close to one of the best geysers in the park.

Distance: 5–7 miles roundtrip

Time: 1–2 days

Starting point: From the overpass exit to Old Faithful on the Grand Loop Road, travel east 2.5 miles to the turnoff very close to Kepler Cascades on the south side of the Grand Loop Road. The trailhead is at a small parking area with vault toilets.

GPS (trailhead): Latitude 44°26'40.69"N and Longitude 110°48'16.35"W

Campsite OA2 is darned cozy as well.

The Lone Star trailhead (OK1) is close to Old Faithful, just off the main road in the Geyser Region. The trail to the geyser is actually an old single-lane service road that is paved but still feels rustic. The road parallels the Firehole River through a gorgeous pine forest with beautiful meadows that line the banks of the crystal-clear stream in places. Because the road is in good condition and the elevation gain is very modest, this is a relatively easy 2 miles while carrying a backpack. When you reach the geyser, check the logbook to see when the last eruption was and then use that to estimate when the next one will be (details are in the logbook, but it's roughly three hours). If the eruption is close, you can wait. But if you have time, it's only fifteen minutes down the trail to the first two campsites, both of which are very nice. Campsite OA1 is only five minutes beyond the geyser, at the edge of a large meadow that would be good for spotting wildlife at the right times of day.

From this campsite you could return the short distance to watch the geyser any time you like, go a short ways through the trees to watch animals in the larger meadow, or continue down the trail a couple hundred yards to fish the Firehole River near the bridge crossing. If you continue a bit farther (about ten minutes) down this trail, you will come to backcountry hot springs and vents right beside the trail and soon arrive at the next campsite, OA2. Please remember that swimming in thermal features in Yellowstone is never allowed!

This campsite is right next to a spot with multiple steam vents coming out of the ground, and there are also a couple of small hot springs that border the campsite such that streams of warm water flow literally through camp. These small streams flow into the Firehole River just beyond the area shown in our photo.

Campsite OA3 is another mile or so down the trail, and while we did not make it that far, we have no doubt it is also pretty. Obviously, this area provides several good options for a great experience backcountry camping. The distances are not long, the elevation gain is minimal, and the sights in this area are the type that you can only find in Yellowstone. So get out and enjoy it!

 ## Slough Creek

Distance: 10–14 miles roundtrip
Time: 2–3 days
Starting point: The trailhead is on the side road to the Slough Creek Campground, off the Northeast Entrance Road 5 miles east of Tower Junction. Follow signs to the campground, and just before you reach the campground you will see a vault toilet on your right. This is the trailhead.
GPS (parking lot and trailhead): Latitude 44°56'36.85"N and Longitude 110°18'29.31"W

Slough Creek is a popular hiking area with suitable options for a moderate overnight. There are many campsites along the upper section of the river as you near the northern park boundary, and sites S1–S4 are all within 5 to 7 miles of the Slough Creek trailhead (2K5 at Slough Creek Campground in the Tower Region).

The creek meanders through a beautiful and expansive high alpine valley with Cutoff Mountain behind it making a perfect backdrop. The valley is known for wildlife and the river is known for fishing, so there are good reasons this area is popular. The trail itself is in good condition; it's used as a stock and even wagon trail by an outfitter just outside the northern boundary of the park. As for elevation gain, you do have to contend with a bit of climbing in the first 1.5 miles after you leave the trailhead, but once you reach the stream the trail is pretty flat.

The great views and excellent fishing make this area worth exploring. Ideal itineraries would allow for a day of hiking on either end with a day in the middle to relax and explore around camp.

Keep your eyes peeled along Slough Creek, and you might spot a tiny ruby-crowned kinglet with his crown on display. (NPS/Neal Herbert photo)

 **Heart Lake**

Distance: 15–20 miles roundtrip

Time: 3 days

Starting point: The trailhead is 7.2 miles south of West Thumb on US Highway 89, the road to the South Entrance. The parking area and trailhead are on the east side of the road.

GPS (parking lot and trailhead): Latitude 44°19'2.48"N and Longitude 110°35'53.97"W

This option is on the challenging end of things and is more appropriate for older kids.

The Heart Lake trailhead (8N1) is in the southern portion of the park. It's also in a bear management area that does not open to hikers until July 1, so this trip can only be done in the latter part of the summer. It is 7.5 miles to the nearest site, and the first 4 miles are pretty unvaried as you gradually climb through a mature stand of trees without much change in the view. But once you can see the lake, you're in a beautiful area, and the campsites along the west shore are sandwiched between Heart Lake and Mount Sheridan. From here, the trail loses significant elevation, making it strenuous; but with expansive views for a reward, it's a great day-hike option for those with the energy to do it. The lake, with several small feeder streams entering it, has great fishing. We would plan three days for this trip: a day to arrive, a second day to explore the area around the lake, and a third day to hike out.

The campsites along the west shore are 8H1–8H6, and they can be reserved for only up to two nights. This is a popular hiking area, but not one for the faint of heart.

CAMPING AND LODGING

Trying to determine where you are going to stay in the park can be one of the most difficult and frustrating parts of planning your vacation. You can stay outside the park and drive in every day, but that means more time in the car. You can camp at one of the twelve campgrounds, but some campgrounds (the five managed by Xanterra) accept reservations while others (the seven managed by the National Park Service) are first come, first served. Accommodations are also available inside the park at lodges and cabins, but they can be expensive, and getting reservations can be challenging. Take heart, because we've done the research for you.

CAMPING

Below you will find a brief discussion of what each campground is like. They're broken out by region so you'll know where to stay to be close to the action you have planned for that day. Again, refer to our region map and the Yellowstone Adventures chapter to make the most of your time. We have provided some quick tips, a grid that compares the features of each of the campgrounds, and a key to some of the terms used.

Geyser Region Campgrounds

MADISON. This medium-sized, full-featured campground is in a forested area with ample shade near the confluence of the Firehole and Gibbon rivers, which is a beautiful area. This campground's central location makes it well suited for accessing the Norris Geyser Basin as well as other features of the Geyser Region, including Grand Prismatic Spring and Old Faithful. It offers eight different loops of camping spots; loops

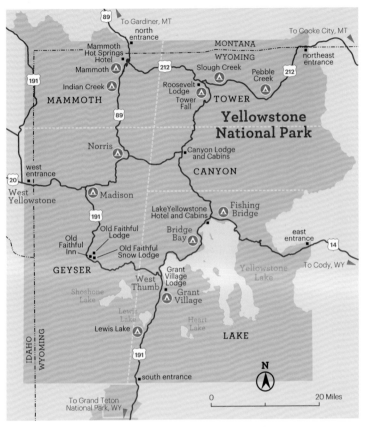

Yellowstone camping and lodging options

A–F are open to both RVs and tents, while loops G and H are for tents only.

NORRIS. This smaller campground is in a beautiful location on a wooded hill overlooking a large meadow with the Gibbon River running through it. It has three loops, with loop A offering the best views of the meadow, as well as some walk-in sites that are just a short distance from where you park your vehicle. It is just a mile or two from Norris Geyser Basin and a short

Yellowstone Campgrounds and Lodges

Region	Lodges	Campgrounds	Reservatio
Geyser		Madison	Xanterra
Geyser		Norris	No
Geyser	Old Faithful Snow Lodge & Cabins		Xanterra
Geyser	Old Faithful Lodge Cabins		Xanterra
Geyser	Old Faithful Inn		Xanterra
Mammoth		Mammoth	No
Mammoth		Indian Creek	No
Mammoth	Mammoth Hot Springs Hotel & Cabins		Xantera
Tower		Tower Fall	No
Tower		Slough Creek	No
Tower		Pebble Creek	No
Tower	Roosevelt Lodge & Cabins		Xanterra
Canyon		Canyon	Xanterra
Canyon	Canyon Lodge & Cabins		Xanterra
Lake		Fishing Bridge	Xanterra
Lake		Bridge Bay	Xanterra
Lake		Grant Village	Xanterra
Lake		Lewis Lake	No
Lake	Lake Yellowstone Hotel & Cabins		Xanterra
Lake	Lake Lodge Cabins		Xanterra
Lake	Grant Village		Xanterra

Dates	Notes	Gas	General Store	Laundry
Early May–Mid-Oct				
Late May–Late Sept				
Early May–Mid-Oct	Also open in winter	•	•	•
Mid-May–Early Oct		•	•	
Early May–Mid-Oct		•	•	
Open All Year				
Mid-June–Mid-Sept				
Early May–Mid-Oct	Also open in winter	•	•	
Mid-May–Late Sept			•	
Mid-June–Early Oct				
Early June–Late Sept				
Early June–Early Sept		•	•	
Late May–Mid-Sept		•	•	•
Late May–Late Sept		•	•	•
Early May–Late Sept	RVs Only	•	•	•
Late May–Labor Day			•	
Late June–Late Sept		•	•	•
Mid-June–Early Nov				
Mid-May–Early Oct				
Mid-June–Late Sept				•
Late May–Late Sept		•	•	•

drive to other hydrothermal areas of the Geyser Region as well as Madison Junction.

Mammoth Region Campgrounds

MAMMOTH. This campground is the only one open year-round, so if you're looking for some chilly winter camping, then this is your spot! If you come in summer like most people, be advised that this campground is in fairly open terrain and therefore gets a lot of sun exposure. Even in the summer, however, the nighttime temperatures in Yellowstone typically dip into the forties, so that early-morning sun hitting the east-facing slope of this campground can feel pretty good when you're making breakfast. Another consideration for this campground is that it's right across the road from the living quarters for much of the park staff, so your views will include not only the mountains east of

Mammoth campsite (NPS/D. Renkin photo)

QUICK CAMPGROUND TIPS

Always spend your first night in the park at a reserved campground or lodge. That way you won't feel rushed by the pressure of wondering if you will get a spot as you're making your way into the park.

If you're going for a first come, first served campground, get there early to ensure a spot. The day before you go, ask a ranger what time the campground filled the previous day. Staff at most visitor centers and even some entrances either post this information or will tell you if you ask.

The NPS-managed campgrounds that are first come, first served don't have showers or laundry services. For longer trips you might want to stay at a Xanterra campground every few days to catch a shower and do some laundry.

Most campgrounds offer ranger programs throughout the day in which a ranger will give a talk about some of the unique features of the park. The schedule for these is listed in the newspaper you can pick up at the entrance or at any visitor center. The talks are almost always informative and interesting, so find out which ones are offered where you're staying.

the Gardner River but also a complex of roads and houses. This is an OK spot to pitch a tent for a few days, but it will not have a real wilderness feel to it.

INDIAN CREEK. A smaller and primitive campground in a beautifully forested area adjacent to the creek for which it is named, Indian Creek provides easy access to both Mammoth Hot Springs and Norris Geyser Basin, and it's only a modest drive north and east to the Tower Region or south and west to the Geyser Region. It closes earlier than some of the other primitive sites, which caught us by surprise on a September trip to

Yellowstone Campground Amenities

In order of opening	Dates*	Nightly Fee	Sites	Elevation (ft)	Features	RV Sites
Mammoth	All year	$20	85	6200	A,F,G	Most are pull-through
Madison * Ω	5/1–10/18	$21.50	278	6800	A,F,NS,DS,G	Call for availability & reservations
Fishing Bridge RV * Ω ••	5/8–9/20	$47.75	>325	7800	F,S/L,DS,G, hook-ups	Call for availability & reservations
Norris	5/15–9/28	$20	>100	7500	A,F,G	2 @ 50' (signed); 5 @ 30'
Tower Fall	5/22–9/28	$15	31	6600	V	All @ 30' or less; has hair-pin curve
Bridge Bay * Ω	5/22–9/7	$21.50	432	7800	A,F,NS,DS,G	Call for availability & reservations
Canyon * Ω	5/29–9/13	$26	273	7900	A,F,S/L,DS,G	Call for availability & reservations
Indian Creek	6/12–9/14	$15	70	7300	A, V	10 @ 35'; 35 @ 30'
Pebble Creek	6/15–9/28	$15	27	6900	V	Some long pull-throughs
Slough Creek	6/15–10/7	$15	23	6250	V	14 @ 30', walk through first to assess sites
Lewis Lake	6/15–11/1	$15	85	7800	V	All @ 25' or less
Grant Village * Ω	6/21–9/20	$26	430	7800	A,F,S/L, 2S,DS,G	Call for availability & reservations

*	Sites you can reserve	V	Vault toilets
Ω	Rate does not include tax or utility pass-through	S/L	Pay showers/laundry onsite
		NS	Showers not included
••	Site with full hook-ups	2S	Two showers included each night
A	Accessible sites available	DS	Dump station
F	Flush toilets	G	Generators OK 8am–8pm

Pebble Creek campsite (NPS/Neal Herbert photo)

the park. We had planned to stay there, only to realize it closed the day we were to arrive.

Tower Region Campgrounds

TOWER FALL. This small, primitive campground is situated in a nicely wooded side canyon near the waterfall for which it is named. Deer frequently meander through the campground, and this region is also a pretty decent area for seeing bears. It's a really nice campground if you can grab a spot, and a short drive from here will put you in the Lamar Valley, with all of its hiking and wildlife-viewing possibilities. It is also very close to a general store in case you need to resupply.

PEBBLE CREEK. Pebble Creek Campground is in the far northeast corner of the park, near the entrance from Cooke City. It is small in size and primitive in terms of features, but it is in a beautiful spot on the banks of its namesake creek, with a smaller stream running seasonally through the center of the campground. It is pleasantly treed, with nice views of the surrounding mountains, and its location makes it a great place for observing wildlife in the Lamar Valley and the Tower Region. However, it also makes for a long drive to most any other part of the park.

SLOUGH CREEK. It may come as a surprise that this small and primitive campsite is one of the more difficult campgrounds in which to secure a site. It is in the northeast portion of the park, near the Tower–Roosevelt Junction and the Lamar Valley, on the banks of the creek from which it derives its name. The creek is part of the reason for its popularity: anglers often come to sample the excellent fishing here. Likewise, a hiking trail that follows the current downstream is quite popular and a good place to spot wildlife. Finally, some of the more observable wolf packs are known to frequent this area, and it is common to see groups of people at the intersection with the main road, scanning the horizon with massive binoculars and spotting scopes for a glimpse of these iconic animals.

Slough Creek campsite (NPS/D. Renkin photo)

For all these reasons and the fact that it is simply a beautiful campground (none of the sites are very far from the water), if you enjoy primitive camping and can secure a spot here, you will not be disappointed.

Canyon Region Campgrounds

CANYON. Canyon Village, where this medium-sized campground is located, is a large complex with all the amenities. The village is close to one of the park's must-see attractions: the Grand Canyon of the Yellowstone. In fact, the road that services the north rim of the canyon actually exits through the campground. The campground is heavily treed so that only dappled sunlight makes it through the canopy to the forest floor. It has many small campsite loops, all similar in nature. The campground's central location makes it a good base camp for accessing a large swath of the park. In addition to the Grand Canyon of the Yellowstone, which is almost at your doorstep, from this campground it's just 12 miles to Norris Geyser Basin, a short drive to the Hayden Valley, and a modest and beautiful drive to the Tower Region and the Lamar Valley.

Canyon Campground (NPS/D. Renkin photo)

Lake Region Campgrounds

FISHING BRIDGE RV PARK. There is only one Yellowstone campground limited to hard-sided RVs, meaning no tents or pop-up canvas trailers are allowed, and this is it. It offers full hook-ups and a large number of sites in a location on the north side of Yellowstone Lake near Fishing Bridge (thus the name). If you have an RV, this is a good base for lake activities as well as access to Hayden Valley and the Grand Canyon of the Yellowstone, both of which are a short drive away.

BRIDGE BAY. Bridge Bay, a very large and full-featured campground right on the northeast shore of Yellowstone Lake, can be divided into two basic areas. The lower section, closer to the lake, is composed of loops A–D in an area that is mostly open, with few trees. Because it is close to the lake, it tends to develop an afternoon onshore breeze that often becomes strong enough to blow tents over and even snap tent poles. As a result, this area is recommended more for RVs and fifth-wheel trailers. Loops E–J are situated more in the trees and farther from the lake, so they are better suited to tents since the trees act as windbreaks (but your tent should still be well staked to the ground). One

Bridge Bay Campground (NPS/D. Renkin photo)

inconvenience is that the showers and laundry for this campground are at Fishing Bridge, approximately 5 miles away. The campground's location makes it a good launching point for all of the lake activities as well as forays to Hayden Valley and the Grand Canyon of the Yellowstone, however.

LEWIS LAKE. Modestly sized primitive campground Lewis Lake is nestled in a picturesque spot along the shore of its namesake lake in the southernmost section of the park. It is quite close to the South Entrance and adjacent to Grand Teton National Park, which makes it a good entrance or exit spot for those traveling in or out from the south. Lewis Lake is also connected to Shoshone Lake via a navigable river that provides unique canoeing or kayaking opportunities, and a popular but moderately strenuous hiking trail to Heart Lake leaves from the immediate area. The campground is also quite close to the southwestern shores of Yellowstone Lake and a modest drive from Old Faithful.

GRANT VILLAGE. Like Bridge Bay, Grant Village is a large and full-featured campsite on the shores of Yellowstone Lake; the two are about 15 miles from each other. However, Grant's campsites are better treed while still maintaining beautiful views of the lake, especially from loops E, F, G, H, and I. This is the first reserveable campsite you will reach if you're coming in from Grand Teton and the south, and it provides quick access to all areas of Yellowstone Lake and is a short drive to Old Faithful and the Geyser Region. It's therefore well suited to being your first or last night in the park, and it's a pretty nice place to stay even though it's large.

LODGES AND CABINS

All of the lodges and cabins in the park are operated by private contractor Xanterra Parks & Resorts and can be reserved on their website (see Resources). Most lodges offer a variety of rooms ranging from more luxurious suites all the way down to basic rooms with shared restroom facilities, but it's worth noting that none of them have televisions, radios, or air conditioning, as the intent is for the park to remain rustic. Some locations also offer cabins with varying amenities; some of them are stand-alone, while others are grouped together in small units with shared walls. Check the Xanterra website to see the full range of offerings and prices for lodging, but here is a brief overview of each location to help get you started in the right direction.

Geyser Region

There are three distinct lodge options in the Old Faithful village.

OLD FAITHFUL INN. This amazing building was completed in 1904 out of logs and stone from the surrounding area, and it is the biggest log structure in the world. Registered as a national historic landmark, the huge wooden building is worth checking out when you go to see Old Faithful. It offers at least seven different levels of rooms, some of which have a clear view of the famous geyser right out the window—a view you will pay for! The inn includes a full-service restaurant, a lounge, a snack bar, a gift shop, and daily tours.

Old Faithful Inn (NPS/D. Renkin photo)

OLD FAITHFUL SNOW LODGE AND CABINS. One of the most modern structures in the park, this lodge was completed in 1999 as a full-service hotel and won the Cody Award for Western Design. It is constructed of heavy timber, with exterior log columns and a cedar shake roof. Inside the lodge you will find a full-service dining room as well as a faster service grill and a gift store.

The cabins come in two varieties. Western cabins are in groups of four and have larger rooms with queen-sized beds and a full bathroom. Frontier cabins are duplex style, with one or two double beds, a toilet, a shower, and a sink.

OLD FAITHFUL LODGE CABINS. The main lodge was built in the 1920s and has a lobby area featuring a bakery, a food court, and fantastic views of the geyser. The housing units are divided into two options, Frontier cabins and budget cabins. The former include shower, toilet, and sink, with one or two double beds, while budget cabins have only a sink and one or two double beds, with a communal shower and toilet nearby.

Mammoth Region

MAMMOTH HOT SPRINGS HOTEL AND CABINS. This is the only hotel in the park open year-round, and in the summer it's one of the best places in the park to see elk. In fact, you will likely see them grazing on the lawns surrounding the building. The structure was built in 1936 but integrated a guest-room section originally constructed in 1911. It offers rooms (renovated in 2017) and three different types of cabins. The Frontier cabins are like those in other areas, but with queen beds and a bathroom. The unique offerings here are the hot tub cabins, where each unit comes with a private six-person hot tub! These come with a single queen bed and a bathroom. Finally, there is a budget cabin option that comes with a single queen bed and a sink, with communal restroom and shower facilities.

Tower Region

ROOSEVELT LODGE CABINS. This lodge, located near a campsite President Theodore Roosevelt once used, provides the best chance to capture the "Old West" spirit. The whole setting has a cowboy-era feel to it, from the large front porch lined with rocking chairs to the extensive system of corrals that house the stock. From the corrals, guests can take guided horseback trail rides or get a seat in a stagecoach for a tour of the area. One of the most popular options is the Old West Dinner Cookout where diners are treated to a stagecoach trip to a somewhat secluded cookout site where the menu includes steak, baked beans, corn muffins, and other traditional western fare.

The lodging options are also cowboy style, with two types of cabins offered. The Frontier cabins are similar to elsewhere in the park, with two double beds and a bathroom. But the Roughrider cabins are quite rustic and typically contain one or two double beds with wood-burning stoves as a heating source. If you doubt your fire-starting ability, don't worry, because "presto" logs are provided to make sure you get a fire going. Bathrooms are nearby communal facilities with toilets and showers.

Canyon Region

CANYON LODGE AND CABINS. This complex is the largest in the park, offering more than five hundred rooms and cabins. It is next to the Grand Canyon of the Yellowstone in the east-central portion of the park. It offers five distinct lodging options, including Canyon, Dunraven, and Cascade lodges, as well as cabins, a full-service restaurant, a cafeteria, a deli, and a gift store.

Canyon used to offer two levels of cabins, but the smaller Frontier units were removed in 2014 and 2015 to be replaced by two newer lodges that now offer a wide range of room and suite options. The Western cabins that remain are recently renovated and have two queen beds with full private bathrooms.

Lake Region

GRANT VILLAGE. Grant Village offers six two-story buildings with fifty rooms each. These were constructed in 1984, so they are a bit more modern than some of the older facilities. The village offers a lounge, a gift store, and two dining options: a full-service restaurant and a lakeside restaurant with a more casual menu. There are two room offerings in the lodges, premium and standard. Both have double beds and private bathrooms, but the premium rooms also have activity tables, coffeemakers, and refrigerators.

There are two lodging options in the Lake Village area on the western shores of Yellowstone Lake.

LAKE YELLOWSTONE HOTEL AND CABINS. One of the oldest structures in the park, the Colonial Revival–style Lake Yellowstone Hotel opened in 1891 and is now listed in the National Register of Historic Places. This lodge is definitely on the upper end of things, with massive white columns and a string quartet welcoming you as you check in! It offers amazing views of the lake, a dining room, a bar, and a deli. In 2014 the entire building went through a multimillion-dollar renovation, and the hotel now offers, for a fee, internet service and a business center. It has eight different levels of rooms above $300 but also offers Frontier cabins at prices similar to other lodges.

LAKE LODGE CABINS. The main lodge has a large porch well suited for sitting and viewing the lake. Behind this lodge are a large number of cabins that come in three types. The least expensive are the Pioneer cabins, built in the 1920s, which feature one or two double beds along with showers, toilets, and sinks. At the next price and amenity level are the Frontier cabins, which offer the same amenities but were recently renovated. The final option is the Western cabins, grouped in modules of four or six. These are more spacious and modern, with private bathrooms and two queen beds.

SAFETY IN THE PARK

Millions of people enjoy Yellowstone every year with no problems, so you shouldn't feel worried about visiting this amazing place. On the other hand, the park is still fundamentally a wild place, so it should be respected, and simple steps should be taken to avoid being one of the few people who do have an incident when they visit the park.

SERVICES

Nobody likes to think about bad things happening on their big vacation, but they can and do happen. It's better to think, plan, and prepare in advance rather than push aside bad thoughts and hope for the best. In the unfortunate event that you run into trouble while in Yellowstone, the table below lists where to find some help.

Be advised that not all of these services are open year-round, and each venue opens and closes at different times throughout

Region	Visitor Info	Med Clinic	Service Station	General Store	Specialty Store	Gift Shop
Canyon	•		G, W, R, L	•	C	•
Fishing Bridge	•		G, W, R, L	•		
Grant/W Thumb	•		G, W, R, L	•	M	•
Lake/Br. Bay		•		•	C	•
Mammoth	•	•	G, L	•		•
Norris	•					
Old Faithful	•	•	G, W, R, L	•		•
Tower-Roosevelt			G, L	•	M	•
Madison	•					

Key: G = Gas, W = Wrecker, R = Repair, L = LP Gas, C = Camping Supplies, M = Mini Store the year. If you are visiting during the shoulder seasons, in spring or fall, check the National Park Service newspaper you picked up at the entrance or visitor center for specific and up-to-date information. You can also find current information on the Yellowstone National Park website.

We remember one trip when, on our first day in the park, we realized one of our tires was slowly leaking air—so much so that we couldn't drive more than thirty minutes without the tire being low. Worried that our vacation schedule would be ruined on the first day, we pulled into the Canyon service station first thing in the morning. They patched the hole where we'd picked up a nail and had us on our way again in twenty minutes. It was expensive, but not as expensive as driving back out to Cody and losing a day of our vacation. Problem resolved, we continued our trip without missing a beat.

WEATHER

Much of Yellowstone is at or above 8000 feet in elevation, so the temperatures can be downright cold at almost any time of year, especially in the evenings. The average low for the summer months is in the low to mid-forties. That is the average, meaning a weather system at any time could bring colder temperatures. We once camped in early September with an overnight low of 17 degrees Fahrenheit! Average highs are in the seventies, with only the warmer days of July and August ever achieving temperatures in the eighties.

You can compensate for the cold by dressing in layers, and you don't need to go overboard with technical gear. A basic, inexpensive fleece jacket is light to carry and offers excellent insulation. Wool socks have come a long way in recent years, and a pair of merino wool hiking socks will not only regulate your temperature but also provide good protection against blisters due to the wool's natural wicking abilities. Another thing to keep in mind is that you can lose a good deal of heat from your head. This means that even a small, lightweight hat thrown in your bag can be a real lifesaver if you find yourself getting chilled.

Thunderstorms

Warmer temperatures at elevation in the summer also mean that afternoon thunderstorms are common, so be prepared with warm clothing and raincoats at all times of year.

Lightning strikes are another concern with thunderstorms. When you see dark clouds forming on the horizon, you need to think about finding shelter soon. Determining distance from lightning strikes is full of old wives' tales, but the speed of sound is approximately 340 meters per second, depending on temperature and elevation. This equates to 1115 feet per second, or 0.21 mile per second. Therefore, if you see a lightning flash and count five seconds before you hear thunder, then you are only 1 mile away from the lightning! Take cover fast by getting off of high points and finding a group of trees of moderate and equal height. Don't be the tallest thing out there, and don't stand under the tallest tree in the area.

WILDLIFE

In recent years there has been an increasing number of incidents with wildlife in the park. It's not that the animals are getting more dangerous; it's simply that people are respecting them less. Yellowstone is not a petting zoo. These animals are wild, and they will defend themselves if they feel threatened. Park regulations stipulate that you must stay at least 100 yards from bears and wolves, and at least 25 yards away from everything else.

There are two types of bears in Yellowstone, black bears and grizzly bears. While all bears should be respected, it is the grizzly that demands the most attention. However, much of the concern regarding bears is overstated. On average there is one bear attack in Yellowstone per year, and there are over three million visitors each year. Those are pretty long odds. Certainly the more you get off the roads and beaten paths, the greater your chances of seeing a bear, and for that reason we

Black bear

always carry bear spray with us when we hike or backpack. We strongly recommend that you bring bear spray as well if you are going to hike or backpack off the main roads. That said, the National Park Service has done a terrific job managing bears and reducing human-bear incidents, and you shouldn't be overly concerned as long as you follow the rules. Campsites have strict and detailed guidelines for how to keep a clean camp; backcountry sites come equipped with food poles or bear boxes; and trails in entire regions of the park (bear management areas) are closed during certain times of year in order to avoid bear conflicts. Check out the park website to read more about bear safety and management.

HYPOTHERMIA

Hypothermia is a condition in which the core body temperature gets too low. We've all had cold fingers, noses, or ears and lived to tell about it, but when your core becomes too cold, your organs can't function properly and you're in trouble. It's easy to think this can happen only in freezing temperatures, but many cases actually occur when it is in the forties or fifties and it's raining. People wearing cotton (such as jeans, sweatshirts, or hoodies) are most susceptible because cotton loses almost all of its insulating properties when wet and takes a long time to dry out.

The symptoms of hypothermia include lethargy, confusion, and weakness. Victims will start by shivering, and they may have noticeably purple or blue lips. As the condition progresses, they will start to lose coordination and become clumsy; this will carry even into their speaking, so they will mumble and have slurred speech. In advanced stages, they become confused even to the point of removing their warm clothes.

Treatment is pretty obvious: you need to warm them up again. In moderate cases simply getting them out of wet clothes and into dry layers and getting them to be more active will be enough to reverse the condition; a warm drink can also help. Get to a sheltered or indoor environment as soon as possible. Indoors or outdoors, you will want to wrap victims in whatever insulation you can find until they are warm again. Jackets, blankets, and sleeping bags are all obvious choices, but even towels, bandanas, hammocks, and tents can be used in an emergency. Focus on the torso and the head, where the vital organs are.

ALTITUDE SICKNESS AND DEHYDRATION

As you may remember from science class, the higher you go, the less dense the air is. That means that as you go higher, the air molecules are more spread out, so a normal breath of air will actually contain less oxygen. If you live at a lower elevation, you will probably notice that you're breathing a little harder when exerting yourself in Yellowstone. Most people can handle the change of altitude up to 8000 feet with little problem. But how will you know if you aren't handling it well? You might start to feel a collection of flu-like symptoms that could include headache, nausea, fatigue, and dizziness. They typically start six to eight hours after ascending to altitude and generally subside in one to two days. Exertion exacerbates the problem, and returning to lower elevations is the quickest fix.

On a related note, cold high-mountain air also tends to be much lower in relative humidity. It's "dry" air. When you breathe this air in to your moist lungs, it's going to absorb the moisture in your lungs and cause you to lose water faster. Symptoms of altitude sickness are often as related to dehydration as they are to altitude, so drink more fluids during your visit. Keep a bottle of water handy and make a point of drinking more than you usually do; you'll feel better for it. Often we find it difficult to get our younger children to drink enough fluids. Although in our daily lives we seldom give our kids juices or flavored drinks, at altitude we choose hydration over concerns about sugary drinks and carry a supply of individually sized drink mixes. Kids can choose their flavor and then add a tube of it to their water bottles. We also indulge in sports drinks for them while we're exerting ourselves in the outdoors.

FIRST AID

A simple first-aid kit is always a good idea, but this is especially true when you're far from help. As we've noted before, Yellowstone is a very large park with a very limited road system.

Medical clinics are open year-round at Mammoth and during the summer at Old Faithful and the Lake Clinic, but it could be a long drive to get there. Having a first-aid kit in your car will bring peace of mind, and if you're planning on hiking or backpacking, a simple first-aid pack should definitely go with you. When you search for first-aid kits, keep in mind that they come in a wide variety of types. You should specify the variety you're looking for. First-aid kits for your car are going to be larger, heavier, and more complete. Those built for hiking will have fewer components, but they will also be small and light enough that you will actually be willing to bring it with you when you go—and if it isn't with you, it isn't of much use to you. All outdoor retailers carry some type of first-aid kit, as do most pharmacies. Find one that works and keep it handy. If you're do-it-yourself types, you can also create your own kit with a few basic items (see our checklist in the next section).

DISCLAIMER

As we say in many places in this book, Yellowstone is fundamentally a wild place. While that is one of its greatest attractions, it also carries with it certain risks. We have done our best to provide reasonable advice and guidance on how to have a fun, safe, adventurous family vacation in the park, but there is no way that we can write a book that is a substitute for the reader's sound judgment. Conditions in the mountains change quickly, and only you can respond to those changes; a book cannot. Every family is made up of members with differing strengths and weaknesses. You know your family, and we do not. So do your research and make your plans, and then make the right decisions when you're in the park and faced with your specific circumstances. We are confident that with the right preparation and planning, you will have a safe and excellent vacation, but we cannot *guarantee* that outcome.

TRAVEL CHECKLISTS

WILDLIFE SPOTTING CHECKLIST
Animals commonly seen in Yellowstone

- ☐ Bison (buffalo)
- ☐ Elk
- ☐ Mule deer
- ☐ Bighorn sheep
- ☐ Pronghorn antelope
- ☐ Moose
- ☐ Black bear
- ☐ Grizzly bear
- ☐ Wolf
- ☐ Coyote
- ☐ Fox
- ☐ Yellow-bellied marmot
- ☐ Jackrabbit
- ☐ Golden-mantled ground squirrel
- ☐ Pika
- ☐ Bald eagle
- ☐ Pelican
- ☐ Swan

Less commonly seen animals

- ☐ Beaver
- ☐ Non-native mountain goat
- ☐ Least chipmunk
- ☐ Gopher
- ☐ Uinta ground squirrel

FIRST-AID KIT CHECKLIST

Here is what we would recommend for a very basic kit, all kept in a quart-size sealable plastic bag:

- ☐ Tweezers. This is for splinters; you may have some already on your pocketknife.
- ☐ Safety pins. These can secure bandage wraps and be used to create arm slings, etc. Get larger ones that are robust—old baby-diaper pins are the best.
- ☐ Bandannas. These can be used for splints, slings, or to dip in water to cool off someone getting too hot.
- ☐ Adhesive bandages of various sizes and shapes
- ☐ Medical tape and gauze bandages for larger wounds
- ☐ Antibiotic ointment
- ☐ Antiseptic wipes
- ☐ Moleskin for blisters. Duct tape works just as well.
- ☐ Elastic bandage
- ☐ Medication. Ibuprofen and naproxen sodium, also called NSAIDs, help prevent swelling in addition to being pain relievers.
- ☐ Antihistamine for allergic reactions

DAY HIKING CHECKLIST
The 10 Essentials

1. Navigation: map, compass, GPS
2. Headlamp or flashlight, with spare batteries
3. Sun protection: sunscreen, lip balm, sunglasses
4. First-aid kit and moleskin or tape
5. Knife
6. Fire: matches or lighter in a waterproof container
7. Shelter: rain jackets at a minimum, a tarp or bivy sack
8. Extra food: sugary and salty, especially for kids!
9. Extra water: water bottles or hydration system, water filter or treatment
10. Extra clothes: jacket, vest, pants, gloves, hat

Other useful items to consider

- Bear spray
- Repair kit: knife or multi-tool, duct tape, twine
- Day pack
- Toilet paper!
- Camera
- Binoculars
- Insect repellent

BACKPACKING CHECKLIST

- ☐ The 10 Essentials
- ☐ Bear spray
- ☐ Shelter (tent, tarp, bivy sack)
- ☐ Backpack with rain cover
- ☐ Toilet paper and a trowel (human waste should be buried at least six inches deep and 200 feet from water sources; toilet paper should be packed out)
- ☐ Ground cloth (to put under tent)
- ☐ Sleeping bag
- ☐ Sleeping pad
- ☐ Pillow or stuffable sack
- ☐ Whistle and signaling mirror
- ☐ Meals
- ☐ Energy food and snack, especially for kids!
- ☐ Stove
- ☐ Fuel
- ☐ Cookset with pot grabber
- ☐ Dishes, bowls, and/or cups
- ☐ Utensils
- ☐ Bear canister or rope to hang food on pole
- ☐ Backup water treatment
- ☐ Spare clothing for number of days and for weather variations
- ☐ Permits
- ☐ Camera
- ☐ Binoculars
- ☐ Hand sanitizer and/or biodegradable soap
- ☐ Insect repellent
- ☐ Toothbrush
- ☐ Quick-dry towel

RESOURCES

Yellowstone National Park Contact Info

Yellowstone National Park
www.nps.gov/yell
PO Box 168
Yellowstone National Park, WY 82190-0168
(307) 344-7381
For recorded info on weather, road status, etc.:
(307) 344-2117

Visitor Centers

Albright Visitor Center—Mammoth Hot Springs area
(307) 344-2263

Canyon Visitor Education Center
(307) 344-2550

Fishing Bridge Visitor Center and Trailside Museum
(307) 344-2450

Grant Visitor Center
(307) 433-2650

Madison Information Station and Trailside Museum
(307) 344-2821

Museum of the National Park Ranger
(307) 344-7353

Norris Geyser Basin Museum and Information Station
(307) 344-2812

Old Faithful Visitor Education Center
(307) 344-2751

West Thumb Information Center
(307) 344-2876

West Yellowstone Visitor Information Center
(307) 344-2876

Reservations and Permits

Yellowstone National Park Lodges
PO Box 165, Yellowstone NP, WY 82190
Lodging and dinner reservations: (307) 344-7311;
in park guest: (307) 344-7901
www.yellowstonenationalparklodges.com
email: reserve-ynp@xanterra.com

Yellowstone backcountry camping information and permits:
www.nps.gov/yell/planyourvisit/ backcountryhiking.htm

Rentals and Tours

Boat rentals through Xanterra Parks & Resorts at Bridge Bay
Marina
(307) 344-7311 or 1-866-GEYSERLAND (439-7375)

Horseback riding through Xanterra Parks & Resorts
Advance reservations: (307) 344-7311 or 866-439-7375

Trail Guides Yellowstone (for trip planning):
www.trailguidesyellowstone.com

Snowmobile and Snow Coach Tours

West Entrance

Backcountry Adventures, (406) 646-9317

Buffalo Bus Touring Company, (406) 646-9564; (800) 426-7669

SeeYellowstone.com, (800) 221-1151; (406) 646-9310

Targhee Snowmobile Tours, (208) 354-2233

Two Top Yellowstone Winter Tours, (406) 646-7802

Yellowstone Expeditions, (406) 646-9333

South Entrance

Old Faithful Snowmobile Tours, (307) 733-9767; (800) 253-7130

Scenic Safaris, (307) 734-8898

Teton Science Schools, Inc., (307) 733-2623; (888) 945-3567

East Entrance

Gary Fales Outfitting, (307) 587-3970

North Entrance

Xanterra Parks & Resorts, (866) 439-7375

Yellowstone Year-Round Safaris, (406) 848-7311

Old Faithful

Xanterra Parks & Resorts, (866) 439-7375

Nearby Services

West Yellowstone

Grizzly and Wolf Discovery Center
201 S. Canyon
West Yellowstone, MT
59758 (800) 257-2570;
(406) 646-7001
info@grizzlydiscoveryctr.org;
www.grizzlydiscoveryctr.org

West Yellowstone Chamber of Commerce
30 Yellowstone Ave
West Yellowstone
MT 59758

(406) 646-7701
www.destinationyellowstone.com

East Yellowstone

Cooke City Chamber of Commerce
206 W. Main St (PO Box 1071)
Cooke City, MT 59020
(406) 838-2495
info@cookecitychamber.org
www.cookecitychamber.org

East Yellowstone Valley Chamber of Commerce
(307) 587-9595
www.yellowstone-lodging.com

Gardiner Chamber of Commerce
216 Park St
Gardiner, MT 59030
(406) 848-7971;
info@gardinerchamber.com
www.visitgardinermt.com

Grand Teton National Park

Grand Teton National Park
PO Drawer 170
Moose, WY 83012
(307) 739-3300
www.nps.gov/grte

Colter Bay Visitor Center
(307) 739-3594

Craig Thomas Discovery and Visitor Center
Moose Visitor Center
(307) 739-3399

INDEX

Credit: Kaden McAllister

ABOUT THE AUTHORS

Harley McAllister works as a project manager but is most alive when he is outdoors, especially with his wife, Abby, and their boys. He has lived in seven different states and on three different coasts, including four years with his family in the Dominican Republic teaching at a nonprofit school. Harley has rafted, skied, snorkeled, backpacked, mountain-biked, and camped in diverse locations in both North and South America. He has spent a lot of time off the pavement and loves to share his passions with others to inspire them to get outside more often, and have fun doing it.

Abby McAllister is a sometimes-harried mom of four boys, an outdoor enthusiast, a kitchen chemist, and copy-cat crafter. Together, she and her husband, Harley, have traveled the world always seeking opportunities to get their boys out exploring nature. When she is not outside, she is busy writing books and blogs that will help other people get their kids unplugged and outside.

Get more travel tips at the McAllisters' website:
www.our4outdoors.com

The colors of Yellowstone National Park's natural features are out of this world. (NPS/Jim Peaco photo)